'Mario Aguilar tackles the central then writings: that frequently elusive balance and action. Aguilar traces Merton's strugg.. .. .., between the social activists who looked to him for support and the more conservative voices in the Church who did not believe issues of justice and peace to be the work of a monk. Merton's greatest insight, as the reader will see in this book, is keeping contemplation and action in a tension where both are necessary and each complements the other.'

Paul M. Pearson, Director and Archivist, Thomas Merton Center, Louisville, Kentucky

'Mario Aguilar is well placed to offer this appreciation and analysis of Thomas Merton's cross-cutting interests in the spiritual and the political, in the religious traditions and non-violence movements of East and West. While Merton's affinity with Asia is well known, this study also explores Merton's interest in and influence on Latin America, especially through his contact with Ernesto Cardenal. Aguilar demonstrates the ongoing significance of Merton's life and writings for all those who are contemplating their place and engaging their faith in diverse contexts and turbulent times.'

Julie Clague, Lecturer in Catholic Theology, University of Glasgow

'At the time of Thomas Merton's death, a group of us noted his conversations with Daniel Berrigan, the contemplative and activist. Our aim was to embody this dialectic, and our motto was "faith without politics is evasion, politics without faith is management". I welcome this new study of Merton's life and work, especially its emphasis on the importance of his contacts with Latin America. It is timely. As, in Western societies, consumerism and greed give way to austerity and reflection, it is time to revisit the biblical values of hospitality and justice.'

Alistair Kee, Emeritus Professor of Religious Studies, University of Edinburgh

***

Mario I. Aguilar occupies a chair in divinity at the University of St Andrews, Scotland. Born in Santiago, Chile, he experienced at a young age, and together with his extended family, the torture and killing of political opponents by the government of General Augusto Pinochet. He found his Christian vocation within the Catholic Church of that time, and has worked with Christian communities in Kenya. He has lived in St Andrews since 1994, and over the years has led a contemplative life, while being involved with human-rights organizations and exiles. His academic research extends to Chile, Colombia, Kenya, Rwanda and Tibet. He is the author of *Contemplating God, Changing the World* (SPCK, 2008). He has recently completed, in three volumes, *The History and Politics of Latin American Theology* (SCM Press, 2007–8), and is currently working on the nine-volume *A Social History of the Catholic Church in Chile* (Edwin Mellen Press).

THOMAS MERTON

Contemplation and political action

Mario I. Aguilar

First published in Great Britain in 2011

Society for Promoting Christian Knowledge
36 Causton Street
London SW1P 4ST
www.spckpublishing.co.uk

The author and publisher have made every effort to ensure that the external
website and email addresses included in this book are correct and up to date at the time
of going to press. The author and publisher are not responsible for the content,
quality or continuing accessibility of the sites.

British Library Cataloguing-in-Publication Data
A catalogue record for this book is available from the British Library

ISBN 978–0–281–06058–0

1 3 5 7 9 10 8 6 4 2

Typeset by Graphicraft Ltd, Hong Kong
Printed in Great Britain by MPG Books Group

Produced on paper from sustainable forests

Dedicated to my daughter, Sara Ann Catherine
(Father's Day, 2010)

Contents

Preface   ix

Introduction: Merton the contemplative activist   1

1 A contemplative teacher   17

2 A contemplative writer   32

3 Writer and activist   46

4 Hermit and activist   61

5 Merton and Latin America   76

6 Merton's final trip to Asia   90

Conclusion: Merton's lessons for today   107

Notes   118

Index   146

Preface

It was in March 1978 that I had the privilege and the joy of making a retreat at the Cistercian monastery in Santiago, Chile. Since then the Cistercian community has moved outside Santiago in order to search for further solitude and a more fulfilling monastic life. However, the wisdom of Fr Linus, at that time novice master, made an impact on what was to become a long journey through contemplation in life. That was followed by a few years of quiet days and spiritual direction at Ealing Abbey in London. There, Dom Bernard Orchard OSB, a learned English Benedictine, led me into the silence of God by suggesting I should read Merton's *The Sign of Jonas* and Monica Furlong's biography of Merton.

It was only years later that I learned that the Cistercian foundation in Chile had been started from Merton's abbey, Gethsemani, in Kentucky. It was while preparing this book that I learned that Merton almost ended up in Chile and was approached about this. Thus, this book was in the making for some time and I am thankful to the editors of SPCK for encouraging its preparation and writing. As the book was being completed I became a postulant of the oblates of the Camaldolese hermits of California, and I realized that my admiration for and closeness to the life and work of Thomas Merton have been there for almost 30 years. I hope that this work makes a contribution to those Christians and non-Christians who search for the same human solitude and ultimately for God. They will find a soulmate and pilgrim in the person and writings of Thomas Merton.

Mario I. Aguilar
Santiago, Chile

Introduction:
Merton the contemplative activist

On his personal reflections about the life of Dom Flavian Burns OCSO, Abbot Robert Barnes OCSO argued that 'the life of every Christian, of every human being, is a mystery. This mystery of life may be the more clearly seen when expressed in the lives of monks, but it is true of us all.'[1] The following chapters of this, yet another, book on the US Catholic monk Thomas Merton argue for the same: in our mysterious journey with God, within families and within society in general, we are contemplative activists because we draw from the face of God in order to recognize God's face in others, and particularly in the poorest of society.

It is the defence of those despised by society and the challenge to established canons of behaviour that made the life of Jesus of Nazareth that of a contemplative activist for change within Judaism, within Palestine and within the relation between human beings and God. It is the same commitment – religious and political, spiritual and human – that made Thomas Merton, a monk of the Cistercian Abbey of Gethsemani in Kentucky, a follower of Christ and an example for others, following in the same Christian commitment within a contemporary socio-political life.

Merton's life remains a mystery, as suggested by Abbot Barnes above, because Merton was a monk, a contemplative secluded in a monastery, with a vow of life stability, somebody who never attended a public demonstration or a strike, and nevertheless had such an impact on the society and Church of his time as well as within present-day Christian commitment to contemplation and politics. Thus, any study of Merton's writings, diaries and letters assumes a twofold dimension: the knowledge of his life and contribution to a period within Christianity and his own society but also a mirror to our own actions and reflections in society today. For it is through solitude that we challenge injustice in society and it is through solitude with God that we make socio-political statements that challenge society as it is now.

On approaching the life and works of Thomas Merton one must be aware of their complexities. They were intertwined to the extent that life as a monk and therefore as a follower of a rule within a religious order of the Catholic Church influenced most of his daily activities and his life as a whole. If Merton is a very complex person and a very complex writer, those of us attempting to write and to interpret him come up with many different 'Mertons' and many different approaches to his contribution to the life of the Church and the issues that preoccupied his contemporaries. Michael Mott, Merton's biographer, has rightly suggested that as Merton's friends and associates gathered in Kentucky for his funeral in December 1968, they were amazed to see people from so many different paths of life around the abbey. Over several days and while talking to each other, they discovered the variety of experiences that Merton had undergone; those experiences are relived once and again by all writers and academics interested in the life of Thomas Merton, and indeed by all readers of Merton's work. Merton's life was his writings and his writings reflected work he was undertaking at particular moments of his changing life. As in the case of Pablo Picasso, Merton would have also told his biographers that 'my work is like a diary'.[2]

Thomas Merton, Trappist monk, writer and activist, known within the Abbey of Gethsemani as Fr Louis, was himself a very complex person. During his lifetime he underwent many personal changes, and during his years as a Trappist monk he influenced many others with his books, his letters and his regular conferences. His dramatic and unexpected death – he was electrocuted by a fan in Bangkok in December 1968 – was consistent with a life marked by extraordinary public statements about God, the Church, the life of a contemplative and the events that were taking place in the USA during his lifetime: from the US involvement in the Second World War to the Vietnam war. By the time of his unfortunate death in Thailand on 10 December 1968, Thomas Merton had become the most important Catholic intellectual in the USA and a revered figure within the peace movement. Despite the fact that he was so active in corresponding and supporting peace activists and those involved in interfaith dialogue, he was a member of the Order of Cistercians of the Strict Observance (Trappists) and had lived as a contemplative monk at the Abbey of Gethsemani in Kentucky for 27 years.[3] As outlined in Chapter 1, Gethsemani was one of the most austere monastic enclaves of the Catholic Church, and before the reforms of the Second Vatican Council (1962–5), even more austere than today, when monks have their own individual room and freedom to correspond with the outside world. At that time and in the description provided by Jim Forest:

> The monks slept in their robes on straw-covered boards in dormitories that were frigid in winter and sweltering in summer. Beds were separated by shoulder-high partitions. Half the year was fasting time. A typical meal featured bread, potatoes, an apple, and barley coffee. Even on such feast days as Easter and Christmas, meat, fish, and eggs were never served.[4]

It was from that life of work and contemplation, for several years as a hermit, that Merton influenced the politics of the USA at the turbulent time of the Vietnam war and in practice showed the timeless possibilities of a complementary life of contemplation and politics vis-à-vis the role of other world religions within contemporary politics and in particular the religions of Asia.

His life

Thomas Merton was born in Prades, France, on 31 January 1915, of a New Zealand-born father, Owen Merton, and an American mother, Ruth Jenkins.[5] Both of them were artists, and after meeting at a painting school in Paris they married at St Anne's Church, Soho, in London. Ruth died of cancer of the stomach when Merton was six, while they were in Douglaston, Long Island, with Ruth's parents. Once Ruth was hospitalized she never saw her children (Tom and John Paul) again. Merton learned of her fate through a letter that his mother wrote him telling him that she was about to die.[6]

After some schooling in France Merton was moved to Oakham, a small English public school (c.200 students) in Rutland, Leicestershire, during the autumn of 1929.[7] While Merton was at Oakham his father came to visit him, but felt ill on returning to London, where a brain tumour was discovered, and he died at the Middlesex Hospital. In their conversation at the school Merton had told his father that he liked the school, which had become a home for him. When the news of his father's death came Merton felt alone in the world and wrote:

> I sat there in the dark, unhappy room, unable to think, unable to move, with all the innumerable elements of my isolation crowding in upon me from every side: without a home, without a family, without a country, without a father, apparently without any friends, without any interior peace or confidence or light or understanding of my own – without God, too, without God, without heaven, without grace, without anything.[8]

After completing school, in 1935 Merton enrolled at Columbia University and converted to Catholicism, a process that he has described in his autobiography, *The Seven Storey Mountain*, a book that has sold millions of copies since its initial publication.[9] His conversion to Catholicism and to any practice of Christianity was nourished by a strong and close group of friends at Columbia University, friends who remained close to Merton for the rest of his life. The atmosphere at Columbia was charged with the possibility of connecting academic institutions with ordinary lives, and in a pre-war atmosphere there were numbers of active Communist students as well as a very strong anti-war movement connected to other European universities such as Oxford.[10] Monica Furlong comments that:

> like the students at Oxford who were, at the same time, vowing that in the event of war they would not fight for 'king and country', because they felt all war was wrong, the students at Columbia stoutly proclaimed in a massive demonstration in the gym that they would not fight under any circumstances.[11]

In 1938, having completed his bachelor's degree, Merton enrolled in the graduate school of English, started work on a thesis with the title 'Nature and Art in William Blake' and began to feel that he wanted to become a university teacher. It was through reading for his thesis, particularly by reading Thomas Aquinas and Jacques Maritain, that Merton realized that some of his naturalistic premises didn't make sense.[12] He attended a low Mass on a Sunday morning and was enchanted by the atmosphere of the congregation, and read Catholic theological books through which he realized that, unlike his childhood experience, the practice of Catholicism was deeply reflexive to the extent that rationalism and academic discussions enriched faith rather than impeded it. On 16 November 1938 Merton was baptized and received Holy Communion accompanied by his friends from Columbia University.

By then Merton had become a very serious Catholic and his considerations to become a priest came through prayer and while in adoration of the Blessed Sacrament. It was one of his teachers, Dan Walsh, a lay lecturer in philosophy, who helped Merton sort out the possibilities of religious congregations and religious orders. Walsh had been to Gethsemani for a retreat and alerted Merton to the possibilities of the spiritual life and the happiness of many who had joined a religious order.

Merton's decision was to become a Franciscan, and he applied but was initially rejected. It was 1941 and the Japanese attack on Pearl Harbour triggered a certain anxiety in Merton to try his religious vocation before being drafted into the US Army. He decided to try his vocation at Gethsemani, while the Franciscans who had actually decided to take him into their novitiate were kept waiting. During the previous Easter, Merton had spent some days at Gethsemani and had loved the experience, particularly of simplicity as described in his autobiography:

> They were poor, they had nothing, and therefore they were free and possessed everything, and everything they touched struck off something of the fire of divinity. And they worked with their hands, silently ploughing and harrowing the earth, and sowing seed in obscurity, and reaping their small harvests to feed themselves and the other poor.[13]

Thus, Merton wrote to the US Army requesting a postponement to his call to join the army and was given a month to sort out his situation.[14] Merton gave away his possessions, burned the manuscripts of a couple of novels he had been working on and took the train to Kentucky after requesting to join the monastery as soon as possible. After a short spell at the Guest House, together with another arrival, he was admitted to the novitiate by the abbot and in a moment Merton left the outside world and became part of those aspiring to become Trappists. Merton wrote:

> at the other end of the long dark hall we went into a room where three monks were sitting at typewriters, and we handed over our fountain pens and wristwatches and our loose cash to the Treasurer, and signed documents promising that if we left the monastery we would not sue the monks for back wages for hours of manual labour.[15]

On 13 December 1941 Merton entered the community at the Abbey of Gethsemani, thus joining the strictest monastic order of the Catholic Church: 'the life in a Trappist monastery was self-consciously rigorous and penitential. The diet was vegetarian, with meat provided only for the elderly or the sick'.[16] The daily prayer life was intense, as already pointed to in Merton's 1941 diary, written while visiting Gethsemani:

> The life in this abbey is not understandable unless you begin the day with the monks, with Matins at 2 a.m. . . . The hours from 2 to 8 (6 hours) are all devoted to prayer, and all pretty much filled up with prayer, by the time Matins, Lauds, Prime and all the little hours (at least in Lent) are said.[17]

Merton's choice was striking because intellectuals and writers usually joined the Benedictines where prayer and study went together, while the Trappists stressed manual work and communal farm work. However, Merton managed to feel at home outside the world that had captivated him before, and while he thought many times throughout his life about moving to another monastery, he never mentioned the possibility of not being a contemplative monk.[18] As a result, his own search for a more meaningful monastic life evolved from that of a medieval recluse to that of a writer, always pestered by hundreds of letters and requests, and always happy to return to his hours of solitude, contemplation and study.

Contemplative writing as politics

Even when he entered the contemplative life at the Abbey of Gethsemani, Merton the writer and poet never gave up his habit of keeping a personal diary, which had begun when he was at school. His beginnings as an aspirant Trappist were recorded in *The Sign of Jonas*, a collection of his diaries from 1946 to 1952 that reflected his adjustment to community life, including sleeping in a communal dormitory, within the climate of the post-war USA, in which vocations increased dramatically after the personal nightmares suffered by US personnel in the campaigns of Europe and the South Pacific.[19]

During that period Merton wrote conversations with his Lord; his leitmotif was eternity and his personal search for eternity. Thus, contemplation as a way of life remained a personal quest for holiness in a secluded atmosphere away from the worldly preoccupations of most Christians. Merton writes:

> there is greater comfort in the substance of silence than in the answer to a question. Eternity is in the present. Eternity is in the palm of the hand. Eternity is a seed of fire, whose sudden roots break barriers that keep my heart from being an abyss.[20]

Later meditations and writings starting in 1956 on more contemporary issues were summarized in a volume with the title, *Conjectures of a Guilty Bystander*.[21]

Merton searched for further solitude after taking his final vows as a Cistercian monk in 1947 and his priestly ordination on Ascension Thursday in 1949. However, the abbot asked him to become master of scholastics in 1951, thus in charge of those monks who were preparing for their final profession, a role that Merton fulfilled until 1955 when he became master of novices. By the late 1950s Merton was already unhappy about the fact that, because of his service to the new monks, he had little time to pray and contemplate. Nevertheless, Merton fulfilled all the community prayer times, took part in the community manual work and prepared conferences and talks for the scholastics and the novices that clearly required lots of preparation and were mostly of a publishable quality. Indeed, between 1952 and 1960 Merton wrote ten books as well as many other pamphlets and essays.

In his reading, study and writing on a wide variety of topics he always asked the same intellectual question with regard to his life as a contemplative monk: 'How can a contemplative monk in the twentieth century not be concerned with these issues?'[22] His topics are numerous and the tapes of his conferences inspiring; however, there were few monks at that time who would have dreamed of achieving such clarity in their writing and so much knowledge about many different subjects.

The stranger in Merton

It is possible to argue that Merton's experience and perception of any stranger changed throughout his life and that the experience of himself and others as strangers shaped his life of contemplation and his politics of the world. I refer to the stranger as the person whom Merton, as a student, a teacher, a convert and a monk, didn't know and therefore to whom he had no social obligations to fulfil. It is clear that Merton didn't have the experience of the stranger in the streets until he moved to New York City and experienced the mass of human beings that he didn't know. Having lost his mother and father, his schooling at Oakham School and at Clare College, Cambridge, made his life sheltered and secluded among students who became in both cases his own extended family. In New York, and particularly at Columbia University, he found others searching for God, and his experience as a convert made him find a universal home in the Catholic Church and a particular home at the Abbey of Gethsemani in Kentucky where he became a Trappist. By the 1960s, within his changing circumstances, Merton found similar concerns towards 'the stranger' in the concerns for the Church in the world discussed and ratified by the Second Vatican Council, while the stranger in other religions, and particularly the world religions of the East, remained Merton's interest up to his death.

Merton's ecclesial experience of the stranger

The monastic experience of the stranger is rather different from others because monks do not have daily contact with the passing crowds trying to get to underground stations, or the homeless begging on a street corner. Indeed, the experience of Merton as a visitor to the Abbey of Gethsemani made such an impression on him that he certainly found his Christian vocation in monasticism because of the immediacy of his experience there of being a stranger who was welcomed within a community that he didn't know and by a monastic group that didn't ask questions about his personal identity or his own likes or dislikes. Some of those strangers became monks, thus in turn they became strangers no more. Within the monastic setting all visitors, passers-by and those making retreats were welcomed by the fact that any of them and indeed all of them could represent the person of Christ as clearly stated in the *Rule of St Benedict*: 'Let all guests who arrive be received like Christ, for He is going to say, "I came as a guest and you received me."'[23]

Indeed, Merton's own personal anxiety came from the fact that he had been told by a confessor that he shouldn't become a priest while his inner core longed for a family, and to belong to God and to a religious community. As he arrived for the first time at the Abbey of Gethsemani the Trappist monk who opened the door for him asked him: 'Have you come here to stay?' Merton firmly replied in the negative even after the monk's second attempt: 'What's the matter? Why can't you stay? Are you married or something?'[24]

Much later and through his correspondence with other Catholics concerned with ecclesial reform, Merton became one of the leaders of a new opening towards the stranger within the Catholic Church. Nevertheless, he also found himself sharing the same concerns of a large number of Council Fathers gathered in Rome for the Second Vatican Council who asked questions about the possible role of the Church in the contemporary world.[25] One could argue that before the Second Vatican Council polemics and apologetics were central to the Catholic experience; thus any possible acceptance of other religious ways of life were considered detrimental to the Catholic truth, and thus ways to be rejected as unholy. In his speech calling a new council in 1959, Pope John XXIII opened the possibility of a 'Church of the poor' in which those who had been considered strangers could be considered part of God's mysterious plan of contemporary life and eternal salvation.[26] By the early 1960s Merton had already experienced the beauty of strangers who had visited the abbey, and he had engaged with many non-Catholics who were writers, academics, mystics and public figures in their own right. Thus, the impatient Merton, who complained about monastic structures and wanted desperately to live the life of a hermit, was not troubled by diversity. Instead, he was very curious about other human and religious practices as well as other religious ways of practising the love of God and neighbour, or a human life of compassion and abstinence without a concept of God, such as Buddhism.

Very few passages concerning the uniqueness of truth, human or religious, are to be found in Merton's writings, including his reflections and meditations published in the mid-1960s.[27] One of these rarities describes his possible cynicism towards truth as an absolute, seeing that as an obstacle to meeting the stranger and those different from him, thoughts outlined within a whole section on thoughts about truth and violence:

> We are all convinced that we desire the truth above all. Nothing strange about this. It is natural to man, an intelligent being, to desire the truth. (I still dare to speak of man as 'an intelligent being'!) But actually, what we desire is not 'the truth' so much as 'to be in the right'. To seek the pure truth for its own sake may be natural to us, but we are not able to act always in this respect according to our nature. What we seek is not the pure truth, but the partial truth that justifies our prejudices, our limitations, our selfishness. This is not 'the truth'. It is only an argument strong enough to prove us 'right'. And usually our desire to be right is correlative to our conviction that somebody else (perhaps everybody else) is wrong.[28]

Merton's opening to the contemporary issues that challenged Catholicism during the 1960s was triggered by his avid spiritual and intellectual curiosity but was supported by the climate of opening to other religions discussed at the Second Vatican Council. There is no doubt that in exploring the stranger, Merton found an affirmation for his own contentment with monastic life; eventually, his solitary life and his search for other ways of encountering God or the monastic experience associated with Buddhism affirmed him in his own vocation. This monastic contentment on the part of Merton did not assume spiritual stagnation but a continuous challenge to the possibility of a non-changeable Cistercian way of life expressed in Merton's unfailing support for other ways of monasticism, particularly those suggested and later implemented by Merton's former novice, Ernesto Cardenal, in Nicaragua.[29]

Indeed, Merton disliked formality and even the formalism of new documents of renewal that were coming out of the Second Vatican Council. For example, during October 1964 the readings in the refectory of the Abbey of Gethsemani included the Bulletin of the Liturgical Commission and the Congregation of Rites related to liturgical changes for the 1965 season of Lent. Merton liked the liturgical changes, but after the reading of such a formal liturgical document asked, 'How can we have "renewal" with such elaborate formalities as this?'[30]

Regardless of Merton's anxieties, the final documents of the Second Vatican Council included major changes in liturgical practice, the use of the vernacular and other new informalities. However, the major shift incorporated by the Council was the immediate change of all strangers into human beings in relation to the Church, even all those not in communion with the Church. Thus, the opening of the 'Pastoral Constitution of the Church in the Modern World' (*Gaudium et Spes*) remains a clear statement, a clear blueprint that makes strangers into fellow human beings, dear to God and dear to the Church, when it proclaims that:

> The joy and hope, the grief and anguish of the men of our time, especially of those who are poor or afflicted in any way, are the joy and hope, the grief and anguish of the followers of Christ as well. Nothing that is genuinely human fails to find an echo in their hearts.[31]

Merton's concerns as a contemplative for the values and hopes of the world had been canonized and supported by the Council

Fathers, and Merton's writings and his own monastic outreach continued to be filled with a deep contemplation of God and a political challenge to contemporary US society arising out of such contemplation.

Contemplation and social text

In my previous work, *Contemplating God, Changing the World*, I explored the possibilities of a deep-rooted connection between Christian contemplation and social and public activity by exploring the lives of some important twentieth-century important figures within Christianity, including that of Thomas Merton. In my concluding remarks to that book I argued that: 'Within this work my main argument is that Merton, a central figure within a history of Christian contemplation, cannot be understood without understanding the contemplative life that evolves out of an ongoing daily contemplation of God.'[32]

Jonathan Montaldo linked Merton's life, contemplation and text when he argued that 'contemplation is the attention one pays to the complex (and very interesting) unfolding of one's life's text as a book that God is writing'.[33] There are many sides to Merton's life and there are many, many volumes of Merton's life text.[34] It is even possible to argue that there are as many readings of Merton as readers. However, a central tenet of this book remains also my strong suggestion: Merton as a contemplative and as a writer was more influential in issues of religion and politics than any other of his Catholic contemporaries. His frequent clashes with his religious superiors happened because in a religious order and a particular abbey that stressed manual work and farming as sanctifying activities, Merton sanctified his days, and mortified his superiors, by being a writer – a prolific, successful and famous writer.

Fr Louis Merton, the contemplative activist, as I call him, had one twist: he changed gradually to become a pilgrim and didn't change to become the monk that his superiors and the general public wanted. This characteristic, found in Merton the writer, reveals the centrality of the only social truism that unites all humans and all writers: change. Change becomes the only process present in all human beings. This fact is not usually grasped by readers of great writers, who in looking for literary consistency miss the possibility of personal change within social, historical and political change.

Thus, when Merton started writing his own memoirs of life as a Cistercian and produced his major monastic works including *The Sign of Jonas*, he could not have envisaged that many years later people like me would read it as a spiritual work. On reading Merton at the age of 22, I remember feeling that it was a memoir that inspired the practice of prayer and contemplation. At that time I was going to Ealing Abbey in London for short retreats, and the late Dom Bernard Orchard OSB gently smiled when I told him about my reading of Merton, suggesting that Merton was not portraying monastic life as it was lived after the Second Vatican Council.

The Merton that emerged after professing his final vows, and particularly his vow of stability and attachment to the Abbey of Gethsemani, was a teacher of novices who resumed writings and conferences about the religious life and wrote eminent volumes on contemplative prayer, always once again using his own experience and, according to one of his Cistercian students, John Eudes Bamberger, later Abbot of the Abbey of the Genesee, New York State (1971–2001), 'aware of the need to treat the whole area of contemplative prayer in a fresh manner'.[35] Many years of novices who were directed and taught by Merton also remembered his ability to make subjects come alive and to write daily many letters, diaries and papers.

It was natural that slowly Merton needed more time to write and became a hermit, occupying an unused building as his cell and his writing studio. Change was possible for him and change was generated not by what he read but by what he wrote. It is clear that as he wrote he recreated religious and political realities, and slowly his letters and writings started to bring more and more interlocutors to the hermitage. It was through writing that he started to influence Christian involvement in contemporary events happening in the USA, so that over the years his initial ecumenical work at the hermitage became a large network of social and political activists.

Merton's posthumous work, published with the title *The Asian Journal of Thomas Merton*, shows a further change in his life: from being a political activist he becomes an interfaith interlocutor, a writer in his own final search for the truth and the experience of writing in order to understand God and the world. His meetings with the Fourteenth Dalai Lama made an impression on him; however, his unexpected death removed any possibility of explaining fully his own search and spiritual discoveries in Asia during 1968.[36]

This work

Chapter 1 explores the search for personal contemplation by Merton and his role as a teacher of contemplation to many novices and scholastics at the Abbey of Gethsemani in Kentucky.

Chapter 2 outlines Merton's development into a writer who found the essence of contemplation in a desperate search for the written word, a development that led to his correspondence with religious figures and activists of his time.

Chapter 3 explores, through Merton's letters, his political activism expressed in his correspondence with those who were involved in the US civil rights movement and those who challenged nuclear weapons and the US involvement in Vietnam.

Chapter 4 describes Merton's change of lifestyle from coenobitic (in monastic community) monk to hermit. During this period Merton searched again for his true vocation but gathered groups of those involved in the peace movement in order to guide them, stressing non-violence and the Christian belonging to a particular Christian community.

Chapter 5 explores Merton's utopian view of Latin America, particularly the relationship between Merton and Ernesto Cardenal and the correspondence that led to the foundation of a lay monastic community by Cardenal in Nicaragua. That community, located on the islands of Solentiname, became a focus for Merton's attentions, and after his death Cardenal and others took part in the Nicaraguan revolution, advocating their Christian commitment to contemplation and political activity on behalf of the poor and the marginalized.

Chapter 6 outlines Merton's final trip to Asia and his encounter with the Dalai Lama, his studies of Buddhism and his general attraction to a continent where, it seems, he finally found peace.

The Conclusion summarizes some proposed lessons for today related to Merton's themes in general and his involvement with the religious and the political in particular. There is no doubt that the influence of Merton remains strong among some sectors of the Christian churches, and this chapter explores themes that could be of importance for Christian communities today; among others: the welcoming of strangers, contemplation and political activism, lives of contemplation, the silence of God and the contemporary issues of nuclear weapons, ecology, global warming and globalization.

It is hoped that these chapters might give particular insights into single areas of Merton (a spiritual kaleidoscope), and that they can be read either separately or all together as units following the chronology of Merton's monastic life within the Abbey of Gethsemani. They are a short study of Merton's writings and, ultimately, my own hermeneutics of admiration for a contemplative life that does not avoid the contemporary contradictions of society, the world and Christianity. On the contrary, it shows God's love and involvement with a paradoxical world that, after all, is God's.

1

A contemplative teacher

This chapter explores the search for personal contemplation by Merton and his role as a teacher of contemplation to many novices and scholastics at the Abbey of Gethsemani in Kentucky from his appointment as master of scholastics in 1951 and during his years as novice master, a role that he took in 1955 and fulfilled until 1965. His role as teacher meant that his socio-political concerns about US policies at that time were also discussed and presented to his students. Many of them, for example the Nicaraguan poet, Ernesto Cardenal, later remembered more about Merton's conversations about public affairs than his spiritual conferences. Merton managed to combine a deep spiritual life with a search for making a difference among those to whom he had access and with whom he corresponded. In fact, he linked the practice of religion with an interest in contemporary politics that was not expected from a monk living in a Cistercian abbey.

Monastic learning

Over those years of leading monastic formation within the Abbey of Gethsemani, there is no doubt that Merton's talent was a gift to his monastic community at a time when there were hundreds of postulants at the abbey, mainly young Americans who had fought in the Second World War. Merton was a dedicated teacher, and the thousands of pages of notes and lectures available in the Merton archives are wholly representative of his dedication to scholarship and to the formation of future priests and monks.[1]

The role of the master of scholastics was to oversee the learning cycles of those choir novices who had finished their novitiate and had taken vows within the Cistercian order and the location of Cistercian life at the Abbey of Gethsemani. Thus, the master of scholastics was the first point of contact for any monk preparing for priestly ordination. The lay brother novices had a different novice master and their vocation was viewed quite separately until the two novitiates were merged in the early sixties. Merton only taught the choir novices, all of whom became priests in Merton's time.

The master of scholastics had also to arrange for readings, classes, lectures and all forms of related learning for the scholastics. The reader must remember that, in an era before the internet, most teaching was delivered through reading of printed books and that an abbey had only a limited number of books; thus the daily duties of a master of scholastics within a limited pool of possible teachers and visiting lecturers in Kentucky were heavy. The years of learning centred around the Latin language, at that time used in the liturgy; principles of liturgy; history of the Church; some patristic studies; canon law; some ethics; and the history of the Cistercians. These classes were actually given by other monks qualified in the particular subjects. Merton mainly taught monastic studies. Fr Andrew Rodutskey taught philosophy and Fr Vianney Wolfer and Fr Timothy Vander Vennett taught theology.

It is a fact that the daily routine of prayers, meals and monastic activities constituted Merton's central activity. However, he also wrote gigantic amounts in his spare time, a daily habit that grew to the point that later was to constitute his central monastic activity. Thus, by the late 1950s Merton was already unhappy about the fact that because of his service to the new monks he had little time to pray and contemplate. I reiterate the fact here that Merton fulfilled all the community prayer times, took part in the community manual work and prepared conferences and talks for the scholastics and the novices that clearly required lots of preparation and were mostly of publishable quality.

Merton's diaries of this period, written between 1952 and 1960, are filled with references to the need to lead a more solitary life because his tensions regarding monastic life and writing were being resolved only slowly. For example, as early as on 13 September 1952 he wrote: 'I have been making decisions. The chief of these is that I must really lead a solitary life. It is not enough to try to be a solitary in community. Too much ambivalence.'[2] Thus, what he expressed finally in 1960 – his wish to become a hermit – was in motion soon after his ordination, particularly during his busy schedule preparing conferences and teaching for those preparing for priestly ordination within the abbey.

Between 1952 and 1960 Merton wrote ten books as well as many other pamphlets and essays.[3] His topics were numerous and the tapes of his conferences inspiring; however, there were few monks at that time who would have dreamed of achieving such clarity in their writing and so much knowledge about many different subjects. Indeed, within the tradition of the Cistercians in North America most of those working at Gethsemani worked the land and kept cattle in order to feed the community. Merton also recognized that manual work was of the essence for a Trappist when he wrote: 'One of the things that every monk needs to feel, for his own peace of heart, is that he is working for a living, and even making a living by the work of his hands.'[4] As a result, the publication of *The Sign of Jonas*, which, as noted, was a book containing some of his diaries as a monk in Gethsemani from 1946 to 1952, provoked some criticism. This was not surprising to Merton even though in 1953, the date of publication of *The Sign of Jonas*, he was already master of scholastics and engaged in intellectual and writing activities. Merton commented in a letter to his friend Mark van Doren:

I had a little trouble with the book within the Order, and it does not appear that I will be writing another one like it quite soon. But that does not matter very much and I do not regard it as strange that Trappists should be surprised that a Trappist should publish a journal![5]

He had had difficulties with one of the censors of the Cistercian order, Dom Albert, Prior of Caldey, who was not convinced that the diaries should be published.[6] Dom Gabriel had followed that recommendation and spoken against the publishing of the diaries, having already had reservations about Merton's history of the founders of the Trappists, whom he had criticized.[7] As a result, in September 1952 the Abbot General of the Cistercian Order had rejected the possibility of publishing the diaries.[8] If another published diary was not forthcoming his writings on religious, philosophical and journalistic issues were enormous and the total of his writings reached thousands of items.[9]

Master of scholastics

Merton's appointment as master of scholastics in May 1951 gave him great opportunities to study and to write, but his initial reaction was that his interest in scholastics was only human. Thus, Merton described his job as: 'something less than I need and therefore – practically speaking – an obstacle – an occupation that complicates my mind too much for the simplicity of God, a hindrance for this life of contemplation'.[10] There is no doubt that Merton's struggle for deeper solitude became part of his lectures and his own discussions with students at the abbey. A restless soul who could plan several things at the same time every day of his life, Merton set out his thoughts on becoming a hermit and even founding a new monastic order at the centre of his diaries of these years, writing for example:

Yet today's thought was perhaps a temptation I can think of at least 5 of the scholastics who would be dying to go with me if

I went to be a hermit. Some have already spoken to me about it. What they want especially is the simplicity of the Rule just as it was lived by St. Benedict.[11]

A striking feature of this idea is that the hermit-to-be was already thinking of being with others, a feature of the commonality and need for companionship of Merton, previously a solitary boy in school and quite independent throughout his young life. At 37 Merton was trying to consolidate his own personal and emotional life and his abbot must have wondered why he didn't just get on with teaching. Merton's diaries of his years as master of scholastics are not as lengthy as they were previously, most likely because he was busier and only able to write when he departed daily for a couple of hours to the shed where he later was to make his own hermitage or to the woods where he loved to be.

The other striking aspect of the above citation relates of course to his own sharing of the possibility of change with his students, something that they most probably cherished but that would have created an atmosphere of inconsistency among the scholastics. If their master was unsettled in the actual manner of Trappist life at Gethsemani they must have felt it, as other monks would be affirming the stability and single location of the monastic life. Once a candidate entered a monastery or abbey he remained there for the rest of his life. Merton's allusions to possible changes were not the norm; however, Merton was not the norm at all for anyone in a pre-Second Vatican Council monastic community.

A letter to Mark van Doren of 11 August 1953 makes clear references to Merton's extra-curricular activities. Some of the scholastics who had left the abbey had been drafted into the US Army and they still wrote to Merton from their posts.[12] Merton mentioned in that letter that he was writing to a young prisoner in Missouri awaiting execution, who in turn was writing poetry and letters to Merton. Merton, once again, showed a pioneer way of accompanying those in death row, a practice that later would be followed by many people through organizations in the USA and Europe, who would not only campaign for the end of the death penalty in some US states but also befriend individual prisoners and write to them periodically.

The strikingly smaller volume of letters during the years Merton was master of scholastics outlines his preoccupation with his work within the abbey. He had to prepare paper work for the scholastics' approval for final vows and ordination to the priesthood, and that included dispensations in the case of those who were too young to be ordained. Within the liturgical rites of the 1950s, that is before the liturgical reforms of the Second Vatican Council, he said Mass for them; he recalled that in May 1953 he got them to put flowers at the altar he was assigned for Mass while admitting that 'usually we are more austere'.[13] Indeed, he led the scholastics in manual work, recalling in his diaries that he had taken 'seven scholastics out to burn cedar brush in the woods, allotted to us as our little portion'.[14] As well as guiding the scholastics he had to care for them when there was illness. One from the Philippines, Fr José, had been working in a minor seminary, and having seen the Trappist *Spiritual Directory* decided to join the community at Gethsemani, but died in January 1953 of Hodgkin's disease.[15]

However, despite Merton's inner conflicts and his ongoing tensions with his superiors, he enjoyed the company of younger men who looked to him as an example and provided enough praise and affirmation much needed by Merton at all times. Even when his moods changed sometimes, even daily, a prayer written on 12 February 1953, almost two years after taking up the job, suggested that he was quite enjoying his life with the scholastics as he wrote: 'I am grateful to the scholastics because they exist and because they are what they are. And I am grateful to you, O God, for having placed me among them, and told me to be their father.'[16]

Novice master

In July 1955 Merton was appointed novice master, a position associated with absolute trust by the superiors of any religious community and one frequently bestowed on monks who excel in their spiritual life and prayer. In his teaching and life, Merton neither believed in the abbey as a place where men escaped from the world and its temptations, nor in forming ascetics denying their body and humanness by becoming monks. Further, he did not see monks as people who could increase some kind of grace deposit for the Church at large. Instead he was a very individualistic kind of intellectual who believed in searching every day for a balance between his private life as a monk and a larger world outside that monks could not and should not despise.

Taking into account these characteristics, Merton's attitudes towards authority and his challenge to an old monastic ideal, one could pose the question: Why was Merton appointed as novice master? He was surely appointed as master of scholastics for his intellect and his academic talents but novice masters have the task of guiding souls into the spiritual journey, and Merton did not have a normative Trappist journey. His own journey was full of self-reflective creativities and contradictions and the desire not to flee *to* Gethsemani but to flee *from* Gethsemani to somewhere else. These contradictions were already clear to Merton in 1952 through his own contradiction of wanting to move away from Gethsemani but recognizing that 'after all, Gethsemani is where I belong because I do not *fit* in and because here all my ideals are practically all frustrated'.[17]

Merton was pleased with the developments of the novitiate and his role as novice master allowed him to come in contact with devout novices from many different countries. In a letter to Mark van Doren he described the community 'as getting along nicely' and the Nicaraguan poet, Ernesto Cardenal, as 'a quiet and pleasant fellow'.[18] Van Doren had been Merton's mentor at

Columbia University and Merton was glad to let him know that Cardenal, who had also studied at Columbia, was a novice under Merton's guidance. Cardenal, later a member of the 1979 Sandinista Government, was at Gethsemani for two years but was advised to leave because of ill health (see Chapter 5).

It was the experience of being novice master that allowed Merton to become more attuned to the concerns of the world in that he listened to the experiences and aspirations of his own novices who had left the world not too long ago. In a way, the paradox here is that Merton always wanted more solitude, but his writings and letters did not allow such retreat from the world, a fact that created tensions with his superiors, who understood the life of a hermit as a fully dedicated life of solitude, silence and a total departure from the world. Teaching was a monastic necessity, study was a possibility for some, but writing in a public way exposed the abbey to the scrutiny of the world and attracted so many visitors, wanted and unwanted, that some of the monastic solitude started to be disrupted.

For most monks and contemplative nuns, writing was a product of study and only a way of life for learned religious congregations such as the Jesuits or the Dominicans. In the case of Merton, it was his writing that guided his worldly involvement and his prayer that guided his inquisitive mind and tireless writing. For him, prayer, writing and involvement with the world were all closely connected.

His preoccupations as a novice master, however, were for the honesty and welfare of those who joined the abbey and who through their period of novitiate discerned their vocation into the monastic life. It is clear from Merton's writings that he didn't care for numbers and expected candidates who wanted to join the Trappists to be fully committed to the search for their Christian vocation. Thus, in the case of a tall basketball player who asked Merton if he should get married or enter the monastery Merton wrote: 'I did not encourage him to rush in.'[19]

Vocations were still plentiful in the 1950s and Merton records 19 postulants from May to September 1957.[20] His sense was that monks should have lots to do with the needs of the world and that they were offering very little to the people in the world.[21]

However, as a novice master he also continued being critical of the abbey and protested harshly about the silence that made noise, referring to a community where no words were spoken aloud, as the Trappists used sign language in their daily communication. The sign language was useful because the life of the Trappists was in complete silence and even the sign language could not be used between 7.00 p.m. and 7.00 a.m., the period of the so-called Grand Silence. In Merton's eyes the monastic life was full of noise and machines, particularly tractors. As a result, monks lived a busy daily life that seemed to betray the ideals of the Cistercian founding fathers.

Merton's uneasiness about noise in the abbey reflected upon his own search for solitude as an honest project for a monk, and in turn this influenced his novices. His need for reform extended to outlining the possibility that the novices have their own chapel with an altar in which the priest would face the congregation, an advanced thought that would come into effect later with the liturgical reform proclaimed by the Second Vatican Council. But Merton, being Merton, complained when the early liturgical reforms arrived at the abbey and the Octave of the Epiphany was abolished and replaced by the 'Feast of the Commemoration of the Baptism of the Lord'.[22] However, Merton liked the inclusion of the lay brothers in the monastic choir at chapel as with their addition 'the singing was strong and full of enthusiasm'.[23]

It is a fact that at the time he became novice master he started a few years of dreaming about the possibility of opening a more faithful monastic community in a Latin American country such as Ecuador.[24] His own vision was based on the forward-looking monastic community of Dom Gregorio Lemercier, prior of the Benedictine monastery of Cuernavaca in Mexico. Merton wanted to visit the community in order to get ideas for his monastic foundation in Latin America. Throughout his diaries he pondered possibilities of foundations in Colombia (near Medellin, Cali or Papayan), Ecuador, Venezuela and even Paraguay with an enthusiasm and a quick change of ideas that years later, and when one reads his diaries, feel frightfully hurried, without much research being done on any of those locations.[25]

A few days after thinking of Colombia for a monastic foundation, and after the arrival of a letter by Kinlock, one of Cardenal's friends, who was growing ipecac root in the jungle by the San Juan River in Nicaragua, Merton appeared convinced that the island of Ometepe in the Great Lake Nicaragua was the place where the young foundation could start, and they could grow coffee, sugar cane, oranges, lemons and papayas on the side of the inactive volcano.[26] At other times he was convinced that Ecuador was the place and wrote dramatic reflections on his own call to holiness through this enterprise:

> If I could ask for anything I liked and if I had first of all assumed it and taken for granted that I asked to be saved and to be a saint, then I would put it this way – that I would ask for the grace in every case and in all cases to be perfectly consonant with God's Will and that if it were His will, that I become a saint by making a monastic foundation in Ecuador and that the community there would be a very happy and simple one that would do much good in that country and everywhere else too.[27]

These states of mind were part of Merton's personality, assessed by a psychiatrist as been able one day to win millions in business and lose it in full the following day on horses. For, on the one hand, Merton seemed to be extremely happy about his life as a monk; on the other hand, he felt the absolute need of reform within the monastic life, and part of this renewal was to worry more about people's socio-political realities rather than machines. On the one hand he felt compelled to flee the abbey and to go to Latin America; on the other hand he reminded himself of his condition as a monk and a religious: 'I have a vow of stability. God can take care of the rest and of my going, if He wills it.'[28]

Later, Merton asked himself if he was restless because he wasn't giving himself fully to contemplation.[29] It was clear from his conversations with his abbot that his superiors did not think that a Latin American foundation was a good idea and they felt it was 'premature'.[30] Also Merton was given the impression by his abbot that any Latin American foundation would be made up of North American monks and not Latin Americans.[31]

Merton kept himself aware of socio-political realities of oppression and poverty in Latin America through the magazines received by Ernesto Cardenal. In the *Revista Mexicana de Literatura* (*Mexican Journal of Literature*), for example, he read Cardenal's poem attacking the United Fruit Company.[32] Merton was aware of the dictatorships in Nicaragua and Guatemala and the power exercised by the US-owned United Fruit Company in supporting dictatorships in Central America in order to prevent the spread of communism. Merton praised the poetry in the *Revista Mexicana de Literatura* written by some young French poets and one can see his own awareness of the politics of the time. He actively searched for South American books in order to continue his preparation for his own journey and monastic life in Latin America.[33]

In particular, he loved Brazilian poets and commented 'no hardness, sourness, artificial attitudes. Great spontaneity, great sense of human values.'[34] Merton was also deeply moved by the poetry of Alfonso Reyes, Pablo Neruda and Jorge de Lima, whom he described as 'a profoundly exciting poet perhaps the one poet writing today with whom I feel myself in deepest personal contact and sympathy'.[35] He also liked reading the Chilean poet Gabriela Mistral, particularly her poem about Mexico and women.[36] At that time Merton was studying Mexican ruins and ancient civilizations and was working his way through Miguel Covarrubias' *Indian Art of Mexico and Central America*, a book he had borrowed from the Louisville Library.[37] Later, he also read about modern Ecuadorian art.[38] However, in the evenings Merton attempted to read some Latin American novels, suggesting that European and US novels spoke of death rather than life; he found narratives of life reading Ciro Alegría's *El mundo es ancho y ajeno*.[39]

As he longed to be in South America, Merton started corresponding with a significant number of people in Latin America, such as the postulant Jesus Enrique from Mexico, who was spending a year in Tepatitlan; Fr Hugo in Costa Rica; Antonio Canedo, a Bolivian seminarian in La Plata; Fray Jaramillo in Bogotá; Fr Amayo in Iquitos; García in Buenos Aires; Josué Gangon and Gomes in Rio de Janeiro; Ferman, a school teacher, in a village in El Salvador; Fr Alacion of Corrientes, Argentina; and Sourain in Viña del Mar, Chile.[40]

He also corresponded with Monsignor Ricaurte in Bogotá, spiritual director of a Colombian postulant, Guillermo Jaramillo, who failed by three days to make his final profession with the Franciscans in order to join the Cistercians at Gethsemani.[41] Ricaurte had spoken to a Colombian bishop about Merton's ideas for a monastic foundation and came through with a couple of empty religious houses that could be suitable for the Trappist foundation.[42] In February 1958 Merton received a letter from Monsignor Urrea of the Diocese of Santa Rosa de Osos in Colombia offering a property of a hundred hectares for Merton's monastic foundation.[43] The Latin American postulants kept coming, and even the Redemptorist Superior in Lima, Fr Fernandes, requested entry into Gethsemani.[44]

In the midst of those ongoing wishes to be somewhere else there were rumours that Merton could be elected abbot in Georgia and he thought during High Mass about that possibility 'with horror'. Typically for Merton, he calmed his fears by reading, and on that day he read *The Third Eye*, a best-selling book by a Tibetan Lama, Lobsang Rampa, who was writing at a time when Western audiences were attuned to the Chinese invasion of Tibet that had taken place after the 1949 coming to power of Chairman

Mao. Merton commented on the book, writing that 'everything centred on death'.[45] It is possible to suggest that these first steps into Tibetan Buddhism bore in him the necessary curiosity to plan his 1968 trip to Asia and to the Indian dwellings of the Tibetan monks in exile led by the Fourteenth Dalai Lama.

By 1957 there were problems in publishing the journals he had written before joining the abbey as two censors agreed that the diaries, later published in 1959 as *The Secular Journal,* would do no harm while two other censors objected to their publication, trying to see them from the eyes of lay Catholics of that time.[46] Merton didn't care very much about these problems; instead his diaries suggest a new awareness that there are those who exploit others, and that silence had become complicity with the oppressors – a problem that, according to Merton, had not been tackled by moral theologians.[47] Merton's response was a personal one that would change his outlook on personal study and reading: 'hence – my obligation to study questions of history, economics, etc. in so far as I can'.[48]

By then his novices started to be influenced by his personal quest and, as he prepared a conference on the First Letter of John about love in deeds, he asked himself: 'is it possible in a capitalist economy to live up to the doctrine of this epistle?'[49] And he asked himself whether it was sinful to acquire a property of 1,000 to 2,000 acres in Latin America for a monastic community, taking into account the criticisms towards the Church made by the Mexican agrarian reform.[50] Further, he asked questions about his being an American, and had a shift from an American as a US citizen to 'an American of the Andes'.[51]

By 1958 the length of his diaries increased, and while he was dealing with the problems of the novices he started recording more and more visitors, including the Nicaraguan writer Pablo Antonio Cuadra,[52] one of the first Latin American writers to visit him.[53] Cuadra visited him accompanied by his wife, and he read poems to Merton including, *El jaguar y la luna* (the jaguar and the moon), a poem that Merton was to translate into English. They met with Ernesto Cardenal and they talked once again about the possibilities of opening a monastery at Ometepe Island in Nicaragua. It is possible to argue that this meeting triggered the increasing practice by Merton of meeting with writers face to face, a practice that other monks would have had restricted but which, in the case of Merton, went side by side with his concern for Latin American novices and postulants under his care.

All of Merton's worries and anxieties about leaving Gethsemani were settled by his obedience to his superiors when a letter from Rome arrived dated 7 December 1959.[54] The letter arrived ten days later and Merton described it as 'a large envelope' that he took back to the novitiate and read on his knees in front of the Blessed Sacrament. He knew that it was a response to his request to leave Gethsemani and to join Dom Gregorio Lemercier at his monastery in Cuernavaca, Mexico. The letter was signed by Cardinal Valerio Valeri and Cardinal Larraona, and it was clear, definite and final. It conveyed the message that his exit from the Trappists would upset many people within the order, and the signatories confirmed the opinion of Merton's superiors that he did not have an eremitical vocation. They requested him to stay at the monastery, where he would finally find 'interior solitude'. Merton felt relief and a finality from the spirit of the letter, and proceeded to head to his novices, who were expecting a talk from him that day. Later that day, Merton wrote: 'I will, of course, answer the letter, and may take the opportunity to explain that my idea was not simply to "be a hermit" – but it will make no difference.'[55] The matter was settled in Merton's obedient monastic life, but certainly despite his assurances it was not settled in his own heart.

In August 1965 Merton finished his term as novice master and finally he departed for a life of solitude outside the abbey's cloister, residing closer to the woods and trying to live the life of a hermit. Instead of avoiding the connections between the practice of religion and involvement in politics, he became ever more immersed in contemplation and in the politics of his time. However, he did so not by changing place or vocation but by returning to his own personal vocation: that of a writer who rearranged his own world and that of others by writing.

2

A contemplative writer

Despite Merton's plans and utopias he remained throughout his life a writer. Indeed, Merton wrote: 'I had always wanted to be a writer. But one had to make a living and so I took up teaching (literature, college level) as a profession that would be favourable for writing.'[1] A writer, I would argue, is not only a person who writes frequently but also a person who through writing outlines and expresses his own life to others. Thus, writers are reclusive people because the act of writing is a solitary one, but they are literary extroverts who bring their own feelings and thoughts into the public sphere. Further, writers are writers because they think about the whole world through what they write and they believe, rightly or wrongly, that their writing can affect others and change and challenge the material world as interpreted by human beings. Writers are born writers and their capabilities, talents and feelings remain dormant until through either reflexive learning or contact with others they start writing, voraciously, consistently, and as a daily way of expressing reality and ultimately their own reality. In the case of Merton the writer, one should add a further characteristic: he believed that his writings interpreted what God wanted for other people and that his writings were implementing also his own search for a world connected with that of God. For Merton searched for the meaning of contemplation and the monastic life through his own lines and books daily.

This chapter explores some of those movements within Merton's life. I would argue that Merton became a contemplative writer;

that is, monastic contemplation and personal writing became one and the same movement within his own monastic life – if others talked or prayed through set formulae, Merton wrote. And in writing he reinvented himself to the point that writings became for him tangible realities to be contemplated. Writing changed him as he experienced the exhilarating results of his years as novice master (1955–65). Through writing he meddled in politics because any writer who publishes makes a public statement of self, of self-belief, of self-politics, and as a result challenges other members of society's perception of self, society and God. This influence, though, could be assumed to be passive and with no particular intention; however, in the case of Merton this activity was a critical and active personal engagement with the world of monasticism and the political world outside the walls.

Thus, Merton had no hesitation in writing that 'we live in prophetic and eschatological times, and by and large everyone is asleep'.[2] He meant these thoughts of critical sleepiness to apply to people inside the monastery as well as within society at large, and he didn't hesitate to write in order to awaken others and make them active within the contemporary religious and political issues of his time. This he did by becoming a prolific writer who corresponded with many people and who managed to communicate well.

The prolific writer

As stated in the previous chapter, Merton was a prolific writer despite the fact that he had to teach as master of scholastics and later as novice master. He wrote daily, not just when he had the time; he deliberately made time for his writing in his busy daily life. However, after he ended his job as novice master he returned to a more dedicated writing life.

In case one misses the point let me outline Merton's correspondence in February 1960 when he was still novice master with only a couple of hours to spare for his own personal activities. From 7 to 13 February 1960, described by Merton as an average week, he received a letter from Bob MacGregor at New Directions, one card from the journal *Thought*, a letter from Jaime Andrade (Quito), a note from Cliff Snow in Louisville, a letter from Perry Knowlton at Curtis Brown, a letter from St Procopius Abbey at Illinois, a letter from a sister in Wisconsin, a letter from Rosa Maria in Recife, and a letter from the Vatican Secretariat of State – total: nine letters.[3] A few days later Merton recorded the arrival of a long letter from Cardinal Larraona, another one from F. Cornford's wife, two or three from J. Laughlin, one from Bob Giroux and one from Boris Pasternak.[4] Needless to say he answered them with long replies. Thus, his correspondence was that of an academic or an administrator but it was only in the summer of 1968 that he had a secretary – and as well as his growing correspondence he wrote articles, papers, conferences and books.

The difference, I would argue, between the writing produced by Merton pre-1960 and post-1960 lies in his awakening to writing and contemplation and his awareness of contemporary politics that slowly became part of his daily and personal life. There is a fundamental reason for this: the possibility of personal freedom and time to write acquired by Merton after he ceased to be novice master in August 1965. Merton's dwelling place after completing his job as novice master was a retreat house planned behind the sheep barn built under the guidance of Brother Clement.[5] But from 1960 onwards, Merton had been allowed to spend a limited amount of time in the hermitage. In 1960, he had turned 45 and after deliberations about his welfare he settled the matter of his future life with the thought: '45 is still young.'[6] His life was still full of surprises and the abbot agreed with the construction of a combination hermitage and retreat centre, Mount Olivet, where Merton started spending part of his day while joining the community for prayers and meals. It was at Mount Olivet that his life as a contemplative writer started to take shape due to his wide interests and his extensive correspondence with other people. Thus, this chapter focuses on Merton's practice of contemplation and writing in the period after 1960 until his journey into Asia in 1968, which is outlined and interpreted in Chapter 6.

Daily contemplation and daily writing

Victor A. Kramer has described this period in Merton's life of several years starting in 1960 as 'intriguing'.[7] This is because in this period Merton managed what he always wanted: solitude. However, instead of being a quiet period of contemplation of God he went deeper into the concerns of the world outside the abbey. During the 1950s he had been at the centre of the study and formation of future members of the monastic community. Thus, the refusal to let him go to Mexico meant in fact that his body remained within the abbey but his spirit, reflected in his writings, flew all over the place.

By 1960 Merton's diary writing increased, so that his entries became more about himself and they became longer. For example, on 25 May 1960 he wrote about his outing to vote in the primaries 'without having the slightest knowledge of the candidates'; he said Mass for the Louisville Carmel; wrote to Monsignor Loris Capovilla who was at that time Pope John XXIII's secretary to thank him for a book on Italian architecture that Merton thought could be useful for ideas about the construction of his hermitage: read a book by Lanza del Vasto that analysed Gandhi and Wardha – and he even remarked that 'I am still not persuaded that the spinning wheels were so foolish'.[8] And finally on that day he commented upon an American intercontinental missile fired from Florida in the Indian Ocean and asked: 'Have we lost all sense of proportion along with our faith?'[9] Truly bewildering, the increase in Merton's amount of writing is remarkable in comparison with his previous diaries while in charge of the monks in formation.

His writing was done in the midst of his life as a monk with its obligations of getting up in the middle of the night for prayer and the different offices to be prayed in community during the day (and night). Thus, on Pentecost Sunday of 1960, a busy day for any religious community, he wrote: 'yesterday, under pressure, finished the galleys of *Disputed Questions* with my eyes stinging.'[10] In the morning Merton, 'with sore eyes', said his office in private, commenting on the sounds of a bullfrog making noises while he meditated at 2.30 and 3.00 a.m.![11] He also heard at that time of the earthquake in the south of Chile, the infamous tsunami of 1960 that destroyed Puerto Montt and other smaller places in southern Chile.[12] This information had been posted on the refectory board, a place where monks found not only news but also a place where information was given about those for whom the monastic community should try to pray.

One of the great influences on Merton's writings was his teacher and mentor at Columbia University, Mark van Doren (1894–1972), who was a professor of English there from 1920 to 1959.[13] In 1939 Van Doren was awarded the Pulitzer Prize for poetry and it was Van Doren who promoted Merton's first book, *Thirty Poems* (1944). He selected the poems and convinced James Laughlin at New Directions to publish them, and even signed the contract on behalf of Merton, who was already at Gethsemani. Van Doren was married to Dorothy and they had two sons: Charles (Charlie) and John. Both of them visited Merton at Gethsemani in March 1954 and September 1957. Mark van Doren and Merton had lunch together in Louisville in June 1956 and he also visited Merton at the abbey in December 1961.[14] Van Doren gave Merton the initial confidence to write and publish.[15]

Thus, when Merton was already starting his life in solitude and was working on his *Disputed Questions*, mentioned above, he sent the longer text to Van Doren along with a letter with his comments about the censors, a phenomenon unknown to Van Doren who, as an academic and writer, was used to peer review, a censorship in its own right, rather than ecclesiastical censorship.[16] For Merton confided in Van Doren that:

> censors have, as one of their unintentional effects, the power to make one more ardent, more explicit, more indignant, more succinct and in the end they force one to come right out and say many things that would otherwise have remained hidden.[17]

In that letter Merton recognized that his view of politics was still naive and underdeveloped, answering criticisms from Charlie van Doren. However, those comments showed that he was becoming more and more aware of his own need to interact with US society and its ongoing involvement in the cold war and increasingly large-scale conflict in Indochina. Merton was already concerned about nuclear missiles and the proliferation of armaments and confided to Van Doren that 'I want very much to say a loud "No" to missiles and Polaris submarines and everything that sneaks up on a city to destroy it.'[18]

Thus, the monk and contemplative continued his quest for spiritual growth and contemplation together with a daily increase of reading and writing and, of course, visits by friends and people who had read his books, phenomena that increased Merton's awareness of public societies with a concrete outcome: more writings arose out of Merton's curiosity, opinions or personal stands on those public matters. Between 1960 and 1968 Merton published seminal and significant works such as *Disputed Questions* (1960), *The New Man* (1961), *The Wisdom of the Desert* (1961), *New Seeds of Contemplation* (1961), *Life and Holiness* (1963), *Emblems of a Season of Fury* (1963), *Seeds of Destruction* (1964), *Seasons of Celebration* (1965), *The Way of Chuang Tzu* (1965), *Raids on the Unspeakable* (1966), *Conjectures of a Guilty Bystander* (1966), *Mystics and Zen Masters* (1967), *Zen and the Birds of Appetite* (1968), *Cables to the Ace*, *The Geography of Lograire* and *Faith and Violence* (1968).

In his own reflections Merton mentioned that he wanted to write less and publish less but his contracts were already signed and his enjoyment of writing seemed to dominate his daily life as he candidly stated: 'There is no question that the activity of writing and the thinking that goes with it all is for me healthy and productive – because, I suppose, it is my most normal activity.'[19] Merton had mentioned in several letters that he wanted to write less; for example, to Professor Hering in Strasbourg he wrote: 'I keep on writing books, too many, though I think I have done enough of this foolishness, and I am planning to stop, at least gradually.'[20]

In August 1960 he mentioned that for an article he was working on he was reading the proofs of *The Divine Milieu* by Pierre Teilhard de Chardin to be published by Harpers.[21] He was recognized as a writer by Columbia University in 1961 when he was awarded the University Medal for Excellence. As the Cistercian rules did not allow him to be present, the trustees of Columbia University agreed that the medal would be conferred *in absentia*, and Mark van Doren received it on his behalf on 6 June 1961.

Two comments are in order here. First of all, Merton was not free to go to New York and receive the medal in person. Second, this recognition must have boosted Merton's sense of himself, even when he didn't see the reason why he was receiving a medal from his Alma Mater. Merton's rationale was clearly outlined to Van Doren in a letter: 'To you it seems logical that I should be getting a medal, then to me it seems logical that you should receive it for me.'[22] The text provided with the medal by Columbia University's President Grayson Kirk must have flattered Merton as it read:

Gifted master of language, in poem and prose, light-hearted as you are grave, you have reached out with winged words to the world you left. In the phrase of one who was your beloved teacher in days on Morningside, you are much less lost to the world than many who insist they are still in it. To his hand, for early conveyance to you, I entrust the University Medal for Excellence as a testimonial of your Alma Mater's admiration and enduring respect.[23]

Merton wrote a thank-you letter to President Kirk knowing, most probably from Van Doren, that the words that accompanied the medal had been written by Kirk's secretary.[24]

Already by February 1961 Merton had a possessive sense of his house in the woods, and he described it as 'the most beautiful little house in the world'.[25] There was no electricity or telephone to the abbey, nor a decent road, but it was clear to Merton that grand plans for building something special were not going through and that a small house was all that he needed for his purpose of gathering ecumenical groups and for his writing and solitude. In a visit to the colleges of Louisville, Mark van Doren had the opportunity to see Merton's house and he wrote to Merton: 'I'll be thinking of you in your little house – but not so little either. I was impressed.'[26] By mid-1965 Merton was already living in the hermitage as he had freed himself of all obligations towards the monastery, though he went there daily for Mass and a hot meal.[27] He enjoyed lots of reading and chopping of wood and was keeping to the times of the community, thus getting up at 2.30 a.m. for his first prayers, looking at the stars.[28]

By 1962 Merton was planning with his editor James Laughlin a book on themes of peace with the title *Breakthrough to Peace*.[29] Merton's hope was that: 'we will be able to go ahead with at least a little of the light of reason, and find our way patiently into some new dimension where war will be a thing of the past', and he continued soberly with the comment: 'It seems unlikely, though.'[30] There had already been opinions by some US bishops against Merton's writings and proposed works and Merton commented candidly to Mark van Doren that 'they would be more at home around the Pentagon than I, and no doubt I would be & am more at home in the pine trees'.[31] Merton had already finished *Peace in the Post-Christian Era* when he was ordered by the censors of the Trappist order to stop the book.[32] *Breakthrough to Peace* went ahead and was published, but Merton's name was removed as editor.[33]

The writer to others

Merton found joy in writing to others. His responses were not short but were expansive at all times and he volunteered thoughts, feelings and self-deprecatory comments without much encouragement. His correspondence and writings increased when he started his life as a hermit in August 1965 as he had more time to read, write and study, but his daily habits didn't change very much as he remarked years later: 'I no longer take for granted that the afternoon is for writing – just because that was the way it had to be in community.'[34]

On 8 September 1966 he took a formal commitment to the hermit life. This new path, much wanted by Merton over previous years, gave him the possibility of structuring his day around prayer, house activities, reading and writing, and immediately after taking up life as a hermit he studied and wrote significant essays on Albert Camus, published collectively after his death in the volume *Literary Essays of Thomas Merton*.[35]

The writer to others had a strategy that worked well: he was personal in his thought and worked through experience. His authority came from the fact that he had been a monk for so many years and what worked for him personally enchanted others searching for the same experience. Lawrence Cunningham has argued that:

> the vast edifice of his personal writings found in the many volumes of his journals or the books from *The Secular Journal* to *The Asian Journal* crafted from those notebooks were quite similar to what the Germans call a *Bildungsroman* – a fiction, which is to say, a construction that traces out the education, development, and direction of character.[36]

Merton's personal touch and experience and his practice of the religious life gave him the authority to treat personal incidents as challenging politics for or against the abbot and for or against experiences lived by others outside the abbey.

Merton the contemplative and the writer followed the daily
routines of his abbey, something that he challenged throughout
his years as a monk. Merton had a few months' affair with a
young nurse (named by Merton as 'M'), and while he argued
that he had behaved like an immature person, there is no doubt
that within his deep concern for the renewal of monastic
life he remained always a monk. None of his literary or emotional escapades were out of character because Merton was
larger than life. Allowing him to be a hermit had to some extent
contained his ongoing search and questioning – but even after
the end of his affair with M he managed to call her. M was
moving to Cincinnati at the time and was crying, telling Merton
that he should leave the abbey and seek happiness. Merton
reaffirmed his commitment to monastic life in his diary entry
with the following words:

> No way of explaining to her that life in some city would be for
> me utterly meaningless. And also that I could not live happily
> with a woman – and that with her it would be a disaster for
> both of us.[37]

It is not always clear how Merton chose the books he was
reading or writing. Ideas came to him, others suggested books
to be read, and it seems that his whole life was spent studying
and writing essays on what he had read. Among the many
books he was reading by November 1967 was Claude Lévi-
Strauss's *Tristes Tropiques*. Lévi-Strauss, acclaimed for his use
of structuralism within anthropology, was at that time publishing his diaries and findings of anthropological work in South
America, and Merton commented, 'he is an intelligent and
fluent writer, sensitive to real problems, ironic, objective, alert,
humane. I like the book.'[38] Merton knew what he wanted to
read and write and he complained bitterly about the many
requests he received, stating that he was 'sick of responding to
requests for articles for this or that collection that someone
is editing'.[39]

A free writer

One of the less explored aspects of Merton the writer was his correspondence with young people – once again let me remark that the amount of letters Merton wrote was enormous, incredible, staggering. He answered letters from youngsters in schools and parishes who wanted advice or a contribution for their school magazines. Thus, when Suzanne Butorovich, a 16-year-old secondary-school student from Campbell, California, wrote to him asking for a contribution to the school magazine, she received not only a reply from Merton but also instructions on how to get letters to him without their being read by lots of people. Merton wrote: 'If you are really anxious to get through and afraid you might not, mark it *conscience matter* and make it look like you are just entering the convent or leaving it or something.'[40]

Boxing Merton into a single kind of experience was not possible; he was a free writer as well as a great financial contributor to the abbey's finances through his writings. When Merton was asked, by a student at Vassar College who was studying 'verse writing', about his group affiliation among poets he replied: 'I would say that I don't belong with any of the groups or schools, and am certainly not involved in the petty orthodoxies of this and that school.'[41]

Following from this idiosyncratic freedom of the pen and work, he advised Robert Menchin, at that time looking to help people who were undertaking career changes, in a definite and very clear manner. Merton wrote to Menchin:

> I would say that there is one basic idea that should be kept in mind in all the changes we make in life, whether of career or anything else. We should decide not in view of better pay, higher rank, 'getting ahead,' but in view of becoming more real, entering more authentically into direct contact with life, living more as a free and mature human person, able to give myself more to others, able to understand myself and the world better.[42]

His sense of a spiritual freedom was also manifested to John Hunt, senior editor of the *Saturday Evening Post*; Merton was extremely frank when he wrote: 'The real inner life and freedom of man begin when this inner dimension opens up and man lives in communion with the unknown within him.'[43]

Already in 1968, the last year of his life, Merton had started a magazine with the title *Monks Pond*, apologizing to Mark van Doren and stating clearly that after four issues as editor he intended to quit.[44] The magazine concentrated on poetry and literature and Merton requested his friend to contribute to this new venture.[45] By mid-1968 the third issue of the magazine was ready to be published and Van Doren had contributed a poem.[46] Merton the writer was happy as he told his friend:

> I am busy, writing a lot, long poems or series of poems [*The Geography of Lograire*], articles: and on nice spring afternoons I run off into the woods and sit in the sun by an, of course, pond. An pond. Hm.[47]

Surprisingly, in the midst of writing about political issues, peace and monastic life, Merton was once again, as he did in Columbia University, working on Joyce and Blake and took pride in telling his former mentor so.[48] In his diary he assumed that Blake would be his desert-island book and he took very seriously this rereading after 30 years.[49]

A contradictory writer

Eclectic writer and forceful thinker that Merton was, writing transformed him. He made authoritative statements to others, particularly on the subject of the cold war after the Cuban missile crisis of 1962, when he started making a clear distinction, not a bar of separation, between 'spiritual' and 'political' action.[50] According to Merton the two concepts, actions, thoughts or ideas should not be separate, but in the concrete reality of the

1960s they had been used in separate ways. Merton's critique of the contemporary peace movement aimed towards a non-violent stand that didn't engage with the consequences of the political. Dialogue was not possible because the peace movement and the Pentagon saw no possibility of it, even when most US citizens at that time were engaged in political action such as voting, and spiritual exercises such as attending Sunday services and praying to God. Merton wrote wisely: 'In terms of politics, I think that the issue is to get down to some real sincere and practical negotiation in regard to disarmament', for Merton did not believe that a unilateral request for full US disarmament would ever work; on the contrary, it would create the conditions for the war machine to justify its rationality against the irrationality of the peace movement.[51]

The writer became an avid advocate of a semi-contradiction: his public opposition to the Vietnam war and his tenet that politics as a human activity was not for him. In his Christmas letter of 1965, a general letter because of the impossibility of answering every letter he received, he confessed: 'I do not see where I can do any good by engaging in political controversy when I am not in a position to keep up with events and judge them objectively.'[52] He remained, though, fully opposed to the Vietnam war but perceived his action of opposition as belonging to the realm of pastoral care rather than direct political action.[53]

John Eudes Bamberger has dwelt on the ongoing contradictions in Merton's life and writings, arguing that Merton was an artist whose style of writing was rather difficult and could easily be misinterpreted.[54] On the one hand, Merton was an artist who expressed himself not as a historian but as a poet and, on the other hand, he was a man who seemed to work on contradictions, literary and otherwise.[55] If during one period of talks he would exalt the figure and ideas of Albert Camus, he could easily, weeks later, argue that Camus was irrelevant in relation to another author. Bamberger suggests that Merton seemed to be for others 'a living contradiction'. Thus, Bamberger writes:

he [Merton] proclaimed, on the one hand, his love for solitude, silence and a hidden life while he continued, on the other, to publish prolifically, much of it quite personal accounts of his life, and to comment on current social problems.[56]

In my opinion, this contradictory behaviour arose not only out of Merton's journey as a contemplative but also mainly because he read and read, and as his intellectual curiosity was being satisfied his interests changed so quickly that his readers and his community found it difficult to follow those shifts. Writing and prayer triggered movements of the mind and the spirit in Merton that didn't provide a single-minded scholar of a single topic but a writer interested in several unrelated topics at the same time.

The richness of Merton the writer and his contemplation of the divine in the world come from his variety of human and divine experiences. Merton is not a single member of a literary club but a rainbow of letters, poems, art, prayers, visions of God and challenges by and to the contemporary world. Therefore, on writing about Merton one realizes that there are different 'Mertons' and that his literary life becomes an endless contemplation of complex processes at individual and social levels. If a stream of ideas was part of Merton's daily existence, his writings opened different avenues of being for himself as the writer, for his correspondents as divine interlocutors and for the world outside, always wanting to steal yet another piece of Merton's mind and soul. For as he remarked in his diary: 'For me what matters is silence, meditation – and writing: but writing is secondary.'[57]

It was Merton the writer who found new socio-political causes, new ideas and new friends through his personal writings and the many letters he generated that in turn led him to meet activists who influenced his development. There is no doubt that Merton had an important voice within the events that were taking place in the USA and by default in Europe and Indochina during the 1960s, the theme explored in the next chapter.

3

Writer and activist

In the previous chapter I explored Merton's gifts as a contemplative writer, a person who while leading a life of contemplation was able to express his own construction of self and world through his daily writing. This chapter explores his political activism, expressed in his correspondence with those who were involved in the US civil rights movement, and those who challenged nuclear weapons and the US involvement in Vietnam, as well as in his own writings. For it was between 1960 and 1962, and coinciding with the Cuban missile crisis, that Merton wrote a series of letters, papers and reviews on the issue of nuclear weapons and the possible use of them by the West and particularly by the USA in the context of the extended cold war between the USA and the Soviet Union. In those years the issue of civil rights for all US citizens, to include Afro-Americans, also preoccupied Merton, as well as the ongoing escalation of hostilities in Indochina. The writer influenced friends who were peace and political activists, but could not avoid having a public influence in those troubled years of the 1960s because he was a well-known, Catholic writer at the time when the Second Vatican Council was taking place in Rome.

The situation of civil liberties and civil rights for all in the USA had already been one of Merton's concerns. His poems, 'And the children of Birmingham', 'Picture of a black child with a white doll' (to Carole Denise McNair, killed in Birmingham, Alabama, September 1963) and 'April 4th 1968' (to Martin Luther

King) bear witness to Merton's preoccupation with the unrest and demands for civil rights in the south of the USA.[1] 'And the children of Birmingham' was written with black children harassed by the police in mind, without knowing that as the poem was being published in the *Saturday Review* four black children were deliberately being blown up in Sunday school. This intention to destroy innocent lives shocked Merton, as did the killing of two other black children who were protesting about the killing of black children. His poem, 'Picture of a black child with a white doll' was his answer to those new killings.[2] Merton considered that the season of Passiontide and Easter felt more meaningful after the assassination of Dr Martin Luther King because they had been in touch with each other and King was planning to make a short retreat at Gethsemani before starting his 'Poor People's March'.[3] One of Merton's friends wrote to him the day before King arrived in Memphis, saying, 'I wish he were going to Gethsemani instead.'[4]

In his writings and meetings Merton was closer to the Christian peace movement, but he didn't ignore the civil rights movement that also included members of the peace movement such as the Berrigan brothers, particularly Phil Berrigan.[5] In a way, the civil rights movement had been preparing peace groups and Christian groups for a very parallel and closely related issue: rights and obligations in US society were intermingled at the level of all rights and obligations, through the actions of civil society and those of the democratically elected government. The 1960s was a time of change in US society because the USA's influence in international policy was clouded by the lack of rights for descendants of African slaves in the south of the country. However, the issues of civil rights, nuclear weapons and the Vietnam war ran parallel, and Merton took part in the writings and the activism/pacifism of all three consequent threats to peace and justice.

Contemplation and nuclear weapons

Lawrence Cunningham has argued in his biography of Merton that:

> Merton's instincts were fuelled both by his own personal debt to his long dead Quaker mother as well as his long-standing admiration for Mahatma Gandhi, but also to his friendship with Catholic activists in the peace movement like Dorothy Day and Jim Forest of the Catholic Workers and his Jesuit friend, Daniel Berrigan.[6] Already by the spring of 1962 an ongoing understanding had evolved between Merton and Dorothy Day who had confided in Merton her feeling that many young people who wanted to help the peace movement had personal situations of unresolved tension and violence.[7] In February 1963, Merton's letter of support to Jim Forest had been published in the Catholic Worker giving a great public boost to the peace movement.

Merton's first article on war and peace with the title 'The root of war is fear' appeared in the *Catholic Worker* of October 1961. The first letters related to the cold war and nuclear weapons began to appear at the same time.[8] This period of the cold-war letters extended from October 1961 until October 1962 and according to Bill Shannon was 'the most vigorous, concentrated, and productive period of Merton's writings on war and peace'.[9] The one-year period was marked by the censorship exercised by the Cistercian order on his writings on war and peace. Thus, the Abbot General of the Cistercian Order, Dom Gabriel Sortais, sent orders through Merton's abbot, Dom James Fox, that he was not to write anything on the theme of war and peace. Merton ventured letters and writings circulated privately and even published two articles under pen names (Benedict Monk and Benedict Moore) in the *Catholic Worker* during 1963. The publishing ban was eased after the publication of Pope John XXIII's encyclical letter *Pacem in Terris* in April 1963, in which he asked serious questions about the morality of nuclear weapons.[10] Pope

John XXIII asserted the need for a general disarmament and a complete ban on nuclear weapons.[11]

Pope John XXIII's statement about peace and nuclear weapons gave hope to many and Merton returned to the issue of his order's censors having forbidden publication of his manuscript. Merton's hope was that if the Pope had discussed this topic and had spoken about a comprehensive ban on nuclear weapons, his own manuscript could be published. However, *Peace in the Post-Christian Era* remained unpublished because the Abbot General of the Cistercian Order wrote to Merton, maintaining that it should not be published precisely because the Pope had already discussed this issue. Pope John XXIII died on 3 June 1963 and Dom Gabriel Sortais, the Abbot General and Merton's censor, died on 14 November 1963. On 22 November 1963 US President John Kennedy was shot dead in Dallas, Texas. As a result, any pronouncement on justice and peace by a Catholic writer was to be measured in relation to the Pope's thought and the ongoing developments triggered by the meetings of the Second Vatican Council. In the case of Merton, his thought went into a series of letters that addressed issues pertinent to the Church in the early 1960s.

In his preface to the mimeographed copies of these cold-war letters circulated to friends, Merton explained that 'the protest is not merely against physical destruction, still less against physical danger, but against a suicidal moral evil and a total lack of ethics and rationality with which international policies tend to be conducted'.[12] In Letter 4 to M. S., Merton outlined the fact that he was not a pacifist; however, he certainly believed that every human being should practise peace rather than violence and that 'nuclear war is out of the question, it is beyond all doubt murder and sin and it must be banned forever'.[13] For Merton saw the problems of an arms race and nuclear proliferation not as military tactics or state policies but as a reflection on the USA as a nation, and his ongoing assessment was not very positive. He described the moment as 'a moral collapse' and the state policies 'more or less frankly oriented toward a war of extermination'.[14] Merton's criticism of the situation extended to the moral theologians whom he described as avoiding self-commitment to anything that they didn't consider 'safe', and he feared that all those supporting war were 'on the brink of a spiritual defection and betrayal of Christ'.[15]

Merton challenged the use of technology and science instead of an immersion into the spiritual world, that world he was experiencing in the monastic life. Thus, some of his cold-war letters were also personal letters to those who sought in Merton some hope, consolation and Christian solace and who in turn gave Merton hope and consolation as well. Merton possessed intensity and an all-absorbing personality that drove him into full engagement with a particular concern, and those corresponding with him gave him a wider picture from outside the abbey. Therefore, if Merton saw the advent of a new year as a challenge to soul, state, nation and Christianity at large, sobering voices from outside gave him the picture of cities such as New York, fully dressed for the celebration of happiness, love, hope and ultimately fun.

After Christmas 1961 Merton wrote to Clare Boothe Luce with an intense sense of darkness related to the escalation of nuclear arms, but at the same time thanking her for some beautiful books she had sent to Merton and the novices, stating that 'what the book gives that nothing else can is the appreciation of all the marvellous detail. It is an unending pleasure for me and for the novices, and we are still wondering at it.'[16]

Merton hardened his position on nuclear weapons early in the 1960s and he was consistent in his complete rejection of nuclear weapons as a possibility for anything that could speak of human or divine justice. In January 1961 he had reviewed the manuscript of an edited collection by Walter Stein, later published by Merlin Press as *Nuclear Weapons and the Christian Conscience* (1961), and had commented that the book, labelled by the editors of Merlin Press as 'hard', was necessary at the start of the year 1962 that Merton defined as 'awfully critical'. Merton expressed it very strongly: 'the debacle is at hand, and it is a question of helping to save what God wills to save, not of preserving present structures that seem to be doomed.'[17] These comments were an extension of Merton's criticism of his abbot and he saw the need to change structures at the level of nation state, Church and abbey.

Consistently poignant in his writings, Merton saw his own position as one of the few who could speak up on matters of nuclear weapons, even when during 1961–2 he was speaking against the position of the US bishops. They supported US policies towards armed proliferation to contain the spread of communism, despite the changing climate already triggered by Pope John XXIII's calling of a new Council in 1959 and the call to build a more humble Church of the poor and the marginalized. At the end of the Second Vatican Council Merton addressed the US bishops in September 1965 with a letter published in *Worldview* in which he insisted once again that 'a rigid, aggressive, and opportunistic use of force will in the present circumstances be not only futile, but harmful to the cause of the West'.[18]

The violence exercised by the proliferation of nuclear weapons was also increased by the involvement of US soldiers in Vietnam and the escalation of violence not only in Vietnam but also within the USA because of protests against a war in which hundreds of young Americans were dying. However, the machinery of war needed more and more soldiers, more and more arms, while poverty and underemployment in the USA were growing.[19]

Contemplation and the Vietnam war

By the 1960s and with the conflict of Vietnam in his heart, Merton exchanged correspondence with the Jesuit Daniel Berrigan and others who had objected to war in general and were exercising their peaceful protests against the draft of young Americans into the US military machine. The US involvement in Vietnam took military shape in 1965 when the first marines landed and, by the end of the year, 200,000 US troops were stationed in Vietnam.

Berrigan first visited Merton at Gethsemani (visit recorded by Merton on 21 August 1962), after they had corresponded not on matters of peace and war but on poetry. It happened that Merton had become aware of Berrigan's poetry, written while he was at Cornell University, and Berrigan wrote to Merton telling him that he was reviewing Merton's *New Seeds of Contemplation* for the Jesuit journal *America*.[20] After the visit, Merton described Berrigan as 'an altogether winning and warm intelligence, with a perfect zeal, compassion and understanding'.[21] By November 1962, Merton was able to write to Berrigan, suggesting that he was reviewing Berrigan's latest book of poems and that he liked it very much.[22] Years later, Merton wrote to friends about his middle way between the shock techniques of the Berrigan brothers (Daniel and Philip), and those who supported war as a Christian duty to the state and some Catholic bishops who spoke of the Vietnam war as an act of Christian love.[23] Merton's position regarding war and violence was very clear and expressed in the following terms in a circular letter to friends in midsummer 1968:

> I am against war, against violence, against violent revolution, for peaceful settlement of differences, for non-violent but nevertheless radical change. Change is needed, and violence will not really change anything: at most it will only transfer power from one set of bull-headed authorities to another.[24]

Nevertheless, Merton objected to the refusal to grant permission for the Berrigan brothers' book against the war to be published, and he even amused himself with the fact that in an edited collection of Latin American writers honouring the Argentinean writer Victoria Ocampo, to which he made a contribution, he had been listed as Thomas Merton SJ (as a member of the Jesuits).[25] The Berrigans' book had been stopped by the Jesuit censors, an action interpreted by Merton as 'the usual fear of someone speaking out and saying something'.[26] Over the years Merton became quite fond of Dan Berrigan and his stand for gospel values, while Berrigan considered Merton a teacher and a friend.[27]

Merton's civil position with regard to the draft for the Vietnam war after 1965 was that of somebody who had previously escaped conscription because of his monastic life; thus he was not prepared to confront the military authorities in the manner that the Berrigan brothers had done by burning draft cards and by spilling blood on files after breaking into federal conscription centres. However, no other contemplative in the history of the USA had had more influence on ongoing political activity than Merton. Some US Catholics distrusted Merton's ideas about the Vietnam war and further they started to distrust Merton's ongoing engagement with the religious traditions of Asia, particularly with Buddhism. For some radicals Merton was a conservative; for those who supported the Vietnam war he was a radical.

If their first meeting took place only in 1962, already in 1948 Dan Berrigan had written to Thomas Merton, praising Merton's *The Seven Storey Mountain*; however, Merton never replied because his abbot had forbidden him to reply to so many letters. By 1962 Dan Berrigan and Merton were exchanging regular correspondence, and the lack of freedom given by Berrigan's superiors for his involvement in the civil rights movement of the South had been discussed. Berrigan was ready to leave the Jesuits and it was Merton who advised him against it, arguing that if he left, many of his followers would not continue striving for civil rights, justice and peace in US society. Due to those tensions, Berrigan was sent to France on sabbatical during 1964, and when he returned he had changed from the well-behaved Jesuit he was before the European stay into a self-assertive, conscious objector to social injustice and violence of any kind – military, economic, social or racial.

In 1964, at Merton's invitation, Berrigan and others came to a three-day retreat at the Abbey of Gethsemani with the theme, 'Spiritual Roots of Protest'. Those in attendance on 17 November 1964 were A. J. Muste; W. H. Ferry (Center for the Study of Democratic Institutions and the Fellowship of Reconciliation – FOR); Anthony Walsh of the Montreal Catholic Worker House; the Mennonite theologian John H. Yoder; Elbert F. Jean (Methodist); John Oliver Nelson (previously national chair of FOR and professor at Yale Divinity School); and the Catholic activists Robert Cunnane, John Peter Grady, Tom Cornell, Jim Forest, Dan and Philip Berrigan.[28] At Merton's suggestion there was to be no rigid agenda and he gave a talk on 'The Monastic Protest: The Voice in the Wilderness'.[29] Dan Berrigan celebrated Mass in English, a ritual Catholic practice that was only fully authorized years later. In 1964 Mass was usually celebrated in Latin. Berrigan also gave Holy Communion to Protestants present at the liturgy, a fact that Merton deemed 'uncanonical' but 'simple and impressive'.[30]

Merton's deeper involvement with Dan Berrigan began on 3 June 1965 when Berrigan, Jim Douglass and Bob McDole visited Merton at Gethsemani in order to discuss Schema 13 and the alterations that were made in the article on war that examined in particular the use of the nuclear bomb by the US military.[31] Throughout the USA a whole generation of youth, mostly fresher ranks at colleges and universities, were questioning the rationality of war and they were reading Merton's essays. Many of those protestors and activists for peace corresponded with Merton because:

> Merton and his fellow retreatants believed that humanity was at a historic moment. A fundamental re-examination of existing values and radical actions was needed. Though Merton declined to participate in person in the revolutionary forces at work in the world, he continued to encourage Gandhian non-violent action.[32]

It was Merton's Gandhian understanding of totally non-violent protest that separated him from Dan Berrigan, a slight separation of means but with common ends.

Historically, the political climate in the USA was becoming more challenging as the civil rights movement changed tactics from peaceful demonstrations to further actions after the shooting of Malcolm X in February 1965 and mass student demonstrations in Washington, DC, against the Vietnam war.[33] In March 1965 the Quaker, Alice Herz, 82 years old and German-born, set fire to herself in the streets of Detroit, emulating the actions of the Vietnamese monks in order to protest against the bombardment of Vietnam. By the end of 1965 another protestor, Norman Morrison, who was holding his one-year-old daughter, burned himself in front of the Pentagon.[34]

Escalation of hostilities by the USA against North Vietnam took place in August 1965 when, after confusing reports of an attack by communist boat patrols against the US destroyer *Maddox* in the South China Sea's Gulf of Tolkin, President Johnson got a Congress resolution that allowed him all necessary measures to prevent further aggressions. US jets escalated the bombardment of North Vietnam. Most of the US voters still supported the war despite the fact that by the end of 1965 6,000 respected academics had requested the end of the war of the US State Department, a body that dismissed the academic cry.

On 9 November 1965, Roger Laporte, a 21-year-old Catholic volunteer at the Catholic Worker House of Hospitality on Chrystie Street in Manhattan, set himself on fire in front of the United Nations Building. Merton sent a telegram withdrawing support for the Catholic Peace Fellowship; however, later on he thought he had been too hard and continued supporting the movement.[35] Dan Berrigan and other non-violent activists had to regain a peaceful momentum as public opinion was moving against those who burned themselves and, in the words of Merton:

Certainly the sign was powerful because incontestable and final in itself (and how frightful!). It broke through the undifferentiated, uninterpretable noises, and it certainly must have hit many people awful hard. But in three days it becomes again contestable and in ten it is forgotten.[36]

Dan Berrigan's words at Laporte's funeral spoke of a sacrifice so that others could have life, and those words ignited Cardinal Spellman's pressure on the New York Jesuits to get rid of him.

The peace movement was at war with the establishment and small actions escalated into full acts of defiance against the state. For example, at 12.30 p.m. on 17 May 1968 nine protestors, seven men and two women, all Catholics, went to the Knights of Columbus Hall on 1010 Frederick Road, Catonsville, a suburb of Baltimore, and burned 378 files (1-A, 2A and 1Y) related to the Selective Service Board number 33 after storming the offices. It took them only ten minutes for the whole raid, and the media that had already been alerted filmed the burning operation, the singing and the praying of the Lord's Prayer that had two central players: Dan and Phil Berrigan.[37] Since 1965 the destruction of draft cards had carried a cash penalty and a possible sentence of some years in jail; however, Dan Berrigan recognized, after long conversations with his brother Phil, that there was no way out.[38] The change had taken place and Dan Berrigan, who had challenged the ecclesiastical authorities with his discourse against the Vietnam war and against exaltations of violence, had changed into a citizen who was challenging the lawfulness of the state to draft into the army young Americans for the purpose of fighting in another country against forces that had not directly attacked US citizens. It can be said that if Merton changed Dan Berrigan into a reflexive member of the peace movement, it was his brother Phil who made him into an enemy of the state.

Merton was not happy with immolation and waste of life and tried to withdraw his membership from the two organizations associated with Laporte. He was also critical of the burning of US public property such as conscription cards, targeted by the Berrigan brothers and other members of the US peace movement. For Merton there were other means of protesting, and the thought of having priests in jail in the USA was not a welcome proposition. Thus, Merton tried to exercise some control over friends in the peace movement, but he failed on two counts: first, they didn't listen to his 'clean' arguments; and, second, Merton was slowly engaging himself in a deeper dialogue with other religions and particularly Buddhism, and thus was not able to gather peace activists at Gethsemani as he had done, for example, five years previously.

Merton had not reached that stage of being considered an enemy of the state before his death, but certainly he was of the opinion that not every war was just, simply because the state executive said so. Would he ever have reached the condition of state enemy? I don't think so. Merton had not had the experience of the crowds and the community reflections that made the Berrigans into radicals and 'state criminals', and while for them there was no way back, for Merton this was not the way.

On the day of the civil protest action at Catonsville, 17 May 1968, Merton was visiting at the Monastery of Christ the Desert, Abiquiu, New Mexico.[39] Merton had been on the move in May 1968, giving a series of retreats and conferences, passing through Nevada and California.[40] There is no mention of the Catonsville incident in his May 1968 diary but he writes about the possibilities of 1968, the year in which the efforts of the USA 'to contain by violence all revolutionary activity anywhere in the world only precipitate revolution. And guarantee that it has to be violent.'[41] One of his last comments in his diary about the Vietnam crisis, before he gave conferences and talks all over the USA and departed to meet his death in Thailand, referred to President Johnson in the following words: 'he has both the clear-sightedness and the fatal blindness of the operator who manipulates for immediate pragmatic ends and cannot see the ultimate human consequence of his manipulation.'[42]

Strong words for a fun-loving, contemplative monk who in his diaries examined life with the spectacle of change and love but who seemed to despise the use of violence by the US government as well as by the peace movement. Nevertheless, in his mid-summer circular letter of 1968 Merton showed his respect for the Berrigan brothers when he wrote:

> it has become 'normal' to regard war – any war demanded by the military – as Christian duty, Christian love, Christian virtue, [so] that a few like the Berrigans, in their desperation, try to show by extreme protest that it is not normal at all.[43]

Merton challenged the peace movement because he didn't agree with self-immolations, risk to one's life, forcing prison sentences on priests, and in general what Merton would consider acts of violence such as burning government property, upsetting workers at government offices and peace protests that expressed violence on others in a public manner. Merton, the writer and activist, was prepared to challenge and influence society but he was not willing to be responsible for acts of violence on life and others in the name of peace and justice. Nevertheless, Merton agreed with other protestors in their analysis of the police and the military as agents of the state, and his opinion was very clear:

> The violence that threatens us to the point of possible self-destruction is endemic in the whole of society, and more especially in the establishment itself, the military, the police, the established forces of 'order' – they are all infected with a mania for overkill, rooted in fear.[44]

If Merton was conscious that protests and political commitment were left to those who led Christians within society, he was also disenchanted by the forceful actions of several members of the peace movement who attempted violence against their own lives and threatened the right to peaceful working conditions deserved by many employees of the US Government. Those employees and not the government leaders had to confront the wrath of the Berrigans and others within their own workplace.

Merton was a catalyst of God's prophetic challenges, he was an intellectual but he was not an activist. It amuses me to think that, while Merton went into eternity in order to know the other world's realities and probably to have longer conversations with God, Dan Berrigan continued his spells of prison and protest, and at the age of 82 he was still being ushered into a police wagon to appear in court for trespassing on military installations or advocating the end of armed intervention in Iraq and Afghanistan. I wonder, as I try to comprehend Merton's writings, what he would have made of the new generation in the peace movement – people, such as the Jesuit, John Dear SJ, who have continued protesting against state violence and the armed race, extrapolating Merton's example as part of the memory and archival semantics of the contemporary peace movement.

In front of me I have John Dear's narrative of his peace action, together with Dan Berrigan, Lynn Fredriksson and Bruce Friedrich, at the Seymour Johnson Air Force Base in Goldsboro, North Carolina, on Tuesday 7 December 1993 at 2 a.m. They entered the base unannounced, an illegal and criminal act, and they looked for the place where the US F15E nuclear fighter bombers, some 75 of them, were stationed. John Dear narrates the scene as follows:

> The plane is waiting for us. The God of peace has set this one aside for us. Bruce and Lynn start hammering the pylons which hold the bombs. Then, they hammer on a guidance light and the lantern all-weather flight pod and pour out of baby bottles their own blood onto the fuselage and into the air intake valves.[45]

I don't imagine Merton agreeing with this act of peace in God's name. The fact of the matter is that the period of the cold-war letters and of personal contact with the peace movement was cut short not only because of disagreements between Merton and those attempting suicide for the sake of peace but mainly because of Merton's commitment to being a hermit. To be a hermit was something rather unusual among the Trappists who had from their initial foundation opted for a coenobitic life of community rather than the life of the more secluded monastic orders of Europe or the more individualistic cell life at La Trappe in France. Merton the contemplative, the writer and the activist searched more and more for solitude, and as he did so he wrote more. As a result he became far more in touch with a world of people out there who needed Merton as much as Merton needed them. An exploration of Merton's hermitic life, the subject of the next chapter, will help us understand more fully what Michael Mott has labelled 'the older Merton' who 'showed a gaiety and high spirits which were largely suppressed during the early years at the monastery'.[46]

4

Hermit and activist

———◆———

In his 1968 pre-Lent circular letter to friends, Thomas Merton defined his life once and for all. He wrote: 'I am committed to a life of solitude and meditation which I hope I can share with others by a certain amount of writing.'[1] However, the road to those thoughts and those moments was not straightforward. Merton had struggled with the notion of changing monastery and community; he had also considered leaving the Trappists and finally had managed to end his job as novice master in Gethsemani and with the blessing of his abbot had prepared himself to be a hermit within the grounds of the abbey. In Merton's candid words it was after he showed Dom James 'Edelin', a wooden, enclosed property close to the abbey donated by Everett Edelin for the purpose of building a row of hermitages, that the abbot got enthusiastic about hermits as a whole. In Merton's words, 'it was because of this that the rest of us got permission to be hermits'.[2]

This chapter explores some of his eremitic motivations and his way of life. They provided a central and ground-breaking contribution to the sense that contemplation and activism within the social realm of political activity (not party-political activity) could go together. Merton was after all a monk and a hermit, and those two charismas within Christianity produced the central nature of his being. The daily practices related to being a monk and a hermit were not fully recorded by him in his diaries or writings. He wrote about what surprised and interested him within his daily routines and the centre of his contemplative energy. His relationship with God remained less spoken and less written about in his diaries and an on-going hermeneutical reading is newly required to understand the rapid changes and paradoxically outgoing development of Merton the hermit.

It is my argument that Merton's life has a lot to offer to the contemporary practice of Christianity because of his search for God in solitude combined with a parallel, full engagement with the public, political and social issues of his time. Merton described himself as 'a contemplative activist' in a preface he wrote for the Japanese edition of *The Seven Storey Mountain*. In that self-definition he clarified that by his monastic vows and life he was saying 'No' to 'all the concentration camps, the aerial bombardments, the staged political trials, the judicial murders, the racial injustices, the economic tyrannies, and the whole socioeconomic apparatus'.[3]

Merton wrote less about God and more about himself and the world. Of course, Merton developed an eremitical experience that was not an easy and straightforward activity of becoming a hermit and staying there without facing other challenges. That would not have been Merton. Most importantly, if his abbot thought that finally Merton would settle as a 'happy hermit' he was also mistaken. Not only did Merton continue corresponding with many people from within his isolation but also he rushed telegrams, had a love affair, and (in 1968) pushed the point of travelling not only within the USA but abroad as well – without forgetting the number of visitors he entertained, his visits to the local library, the meals he took with other people and his own criticism of monastic life as he experienced it before the Second Vatican Council.

Hermits and the Second Vatican Council

Merton became a hermit at the time of the Second Vatican Council (1962–5), when every religious community was asked to reconsider their charisma and apostolate in the light of the Council.[4] This was also true of hermits and those who were part of contemplative communities; all were included in the renewal of the Catholic religious as portrayed in the Council document about the religious life, *Perfectae caritatis*. The Second Vatican Council stated that 'There are institutes which are entirely ordered towards contemplation, in such wise that their members give themselves over to God alone in solitude and silence, in constant prayer and willing penance.'[5] Further, the Council argued for the strengthening of contemplative communities in the following words: 'their way of life should be revised in accordance with the aforesaid principles and criteria of up-to-date renewal, the greatest care being taken to preserve their withdrawal from the world and the exercises which belong to the contemplative life.'[6] Merton's comments about *Perfectae caritatis* were quite direct when he wrote in his diary: 'all this is based on Vatican II, which makes me wonder what is so new about *Perfectae caritatis* . . . The whole thing is sickening. The mechanical, cause-and-effect, official machinery of Catholicism. Dreadfully dead, putrid.'[7]

After Merton's death the Sacred Congregation for Religious of the Vatican published *Venite Seorsum*, an instruction directed to those religious in the contemplative life who impacted on community renewal at Gethsemani.[8] I would argue that within *Venite Seorsum* Merton would not have liked the reiteration of norms of enclosure, confession and penance. In many letters he had expressed the following sentiment:

> Religious life is, I am afraid, so organized and so systematized today that there is a great deal of frustration and development is often slowed down or even blocked to some extent. I think that we should all be praying for a genuine renewal and opening up of new perspectives.[9]

In the case of contemplatives and hermits included among religious, the Council had also expressed the need of renewal in practices and monastic impact on other Christians. Merton had already advanced such a renewal in his way of life, combining a deep contemplation and solitude with his own support for people who sought prayer and guidance from the monastic communities. Merton had been a pioneer of the possibilities that contemplative life brought to society and the world, and he showed that the welcoming of others was not a source of distraction but a much-needed component of contemplative life as required by the Second Vatican Council in its spirit of renewal.

Merton had taken a particular interest in the Council and had first-hand information about the proceedings from Sr Mary Luke Tobin, a Loreto sister, based at Nerinx, Kentucky, who was the only US woman observer at the Council.[10] Merton corresponded with many people about the Council sessions as issues of peace and justice, nuclear weapons and the role of the Catholic Church in the contemporary world were being discussed.[11] First and foremost, he had written to the US bishops regarding war and peace and the possibilities that the Second Vatican Council offered to the world. Note that this letter was written after he had started his full life at the hermitage, and in the letter he urged the US bishops to put love and not power at the centre of the final deliberations by the Council Fathers with the following words: 'What matters is for the Bishops and the Council to bear witness clearly and without any confusion to the Church's belief in the power of love to save and transform not only individuals but society.'[12]

Second, Merton led the way in his ideas of renewal for the monastic life within the Catholic Church, and he took a great interest, not always full of hope, in the possible avenues of renewal proposed by the Second Vatican Council.[13] Merton's collected essays on the renewal of the monastic life, a favourite topic of his, were originally published in 1971.[14]

At the time of the Second Vatican Council, Pope Paul VI wanted a group of contemplatives to publish a letter addressing their communion with the contemporary and modern world and he asked Merton to do this.[15] Merton was not convinced about it, and suggested that as the contemplatives didn't know what to do in their own vocation, they knew even less about the modern world. However, finally Merton decided to write the letter because Paul VI had been personally very supportive of his writings. The final draft of the 'Message of Contemplatives' was the work of Merton together with the French Cistercian André Louf, an outstanding Cistercian scholar and monastic theologian, and the Carthusian Jean-Baptiste Porion, with whom Merton had corresponded since the 1940s. Their letter put forward 'their conviction that it was possible to enter into dialogue with God at an experiential level despite the obstacles put up by modern culture'.[16]

It is clear that the Cistercians of the Strict Observance had started their renewal long before the Council, and Merton had led the way as novice master of the largest contemplative community in the USA. Indeed, Merton's 1968 journey to Asia was made in order to attend a meeting of leaders of contemplative communities in Asia as part of that ongoing renewal of the contemplative life required by the Second Vatican Council.[17] For it is a fact that the Cistercians were a community of common life and that only exceptions within the communities underwent periods of complete solitude in hermitages. In Gethsemani there were three hermits: Merton, Dom Flavian Burns, who left his hermitage to become Abbot of Gethsemani in 1967, allowing his predecessor, Dom James Fox, to become a hermit as well.[18]

There were other communities of hermits rather than monks in community, such as the Camaldolese Benedictines and the Carthusians. When Merton had visited Gethsemani the first time, he had read about contemplative orders in the abbey's library and had decided to join the Cistercians instead of the Carthusians, who also attracted him. The Carthusians were founded by St Bruno who, in 1084, with six companions, moved to a place where they could pray near Grenoble in the French Alps, where they built the Grande Chartreuse. Merton described them in detail in a full chapter of his book *The Silent Life* (1957).[19]

A priest in New York had mentioned the Carthusians of England to Merton. He was enchanted by their solitary ways, as all members were hermits who lived, ate and slept alone and joined the other hermits only for the praying of the office and the communal Eucharist. In the end Merton was unable to leave the USA due to the Second World War. Nevertheless, by the mid-1950s he was still trying to decide whether there would be a more honest and dedicated life for him among the Camaldolese. He wrote to the Italian Camaldolese and was assured that he would be welcome; however, when he applied to be moved and mentioned this to his correspondent, Jean Leclercq, he was discouraged from doing so and his abbot, Dom James, started talking to him about the possibility of becoming a hermit within the land of Gethsemani. The Camaldolese, founded by St Romouald in 1012 in a high valley in the Apennines, organized their cells as separate small huts around a church.[20] They lived in individual cells on their own, did their manual work, some planting and growing of food, and ate alone with the sole exception of the daily Eucharist, which was celebrated communally. Merton had written about them as part of a project that was given to him in his earlier years at Gethsemani.[21] He was to write about the history of contemplative orders, Cistercian holy men and women, and about the history and influences taken over the centuries by the Cistercian Order, a work that was finally published as *The Waters of Siloe* (1949).

In the 1950s Merton had thought of moving to one of those communities of hermits as he had become more and more disenchanted by the noisiness and business of Gethsemani. After the Second World War the abbey had received more postulants and monks than it could actually accommodate, a time that coincided with a full renewal of the agricultural work by monks with the successful introduction of tractors and a modern cheese factory, all part of the modernization of finances and income pushed by Dom James.[22] At that time Merton had been discouraged by other Cistercians and by friends in the Sacred Congregation for Religious from leaving Gethsemani, and he had plotted a journey to Nicaragua with the purpose of founding a new contemplative community with his former novice, Ernesto Cardenal, as alluded to in Chapter 1. Merton had even thought of joining a renewed contemplative community in Cuernavaca (Mexico) that much later was closed by the Vatican because of unorthodox practices that involved psychoanalysis.

Once this process of discernment or disorder had been settled, Merton moved into his own hermitage. Merton's hermitage was dedicated to St Mary of Carmel. It was a small, brick house with a porch beside the woods and within the compound of the Abbey of Gethsemani.[23] By the spring of 1965 Merton was already spending time during the day at the hermitage but joined the community of novices under his charge for prayers and meals, and he also slept in the monastery. On 17 August 1965 the council of the abbey met and appointed Father Baldwin as the new novice master with Merton present. Then, he was asked to leave the room and after a while was told that the council had approved his retirement to the hermitage. Michael Mott comments as follows: 'there was a sense that history had been made with the decision: Gethsemani, the "strictest of the Strict" was to have its hermit.'[24]

One can return to the essence of Merton's call to a way of life he wanted only by citing the belief of the Catholic Church regarding hermits: 'Without always professing the three evangelical counsels publicly, hermits "devote their life to the praise of God and salvation of the world through a stricter separation from the world, the silence of solitude and assiduous prayer and penance".'[25]

Merton's hermitage

On 20 August 1965, on the Feast of St Bernard, Merton bade farewell to the monastery enclosure with an address with the title 'A life free from care'.[26] His novices gave him funny presents and cards and later he went to collect the necessary supplies, including used clothing. Every day he went to the abbey to say Mass in the library chapel and to eat one meal, usually on his own in the refectory of the abbey's infirmary. Regardless of a day of fasting or a day of work, Merton enjoyed one meal that kept him going.[27] His sole obligation was to give a conference every Sunday afternoon, and the abbot had requested that he write a revised manual for postulants. He had what he wanted – but after a week he started feeling lonely in the midst of manual work in the fields that he loved so much and a certain amount of daily writing, an activity that Michael Mott has correctly described as more 'a compulsion than either a vocation or a job'.[28] As we have noted, Merton's diaries do not carry a detailed description of his daily routines or timetables, only of readings he was doing, writings he enjoyed and comments on nature, the changing seasons or the weather. However, he described his daily life as a hermit to the Pakistani Sufi scholar, Abdul Aziz, with whom he corresponded at a time in which Merton explored Islam and particularly the idea of community, prayer and purity.[29] Aziz had written to Merton on 1 November 1960, impressed by Merton's *The Ascent to Truth* and encouraged by another of Merton's friends, Louis Massignon. They corresponded until 1968 and it was at the request of Aziz that Merton described his daily routine and his understanding and practice of prayer.[30]

Thus, Merton described his going to bed at 7.30 p.m. and his rising at 2.30 a.m. followed by praying the office, meditation and Bible reading (*lectio divina*). Then he prepared tea or coffee and read until sunrise. At sunrise, Merton said Morning Prayer and then started manual work until 9.00 a.m. and wrote a few letters. Then Merton went to the monastery to say Mass and ate his only cooked meal of the day. At the time he was writing to Aziz, he had not been authorized to say Mass in the hermitage because in the pre-1972 rite he still needed an altar boy and so on, but he was allowed to start saying Mass there in July 1967. After the meal Merton returned to the hermitage, read and said the office at 1.00 p.m. After saying the office Merton meditated for another hour and then did some writing for a maximum of two hours. At 4.00 p.m. Merton said another part of the office followed by a light supper, mainly tea, soup and a sandwich. After supper he meditated for another hour or two and then went to bed.[31]

The letter to Aziz constitutes a unique description because it shows a clear monastic timetable with little time for writing and correspondence, activities that dominated Merton's life. Merton recognized that he had a hard time keeping this time-table and he was very conscious that time passed very fast in the hermitage.[32] His pastimes were walks around the woods, the contemplation of nature and the use of a record player that allowed him to listen to music that other people regularly sent him, particularly jazz and contemporary songs related to the peace movement and 1960s criticism of authority, including songs by Joan Baez and Bob Dylan.[33] He enjoyed listening to some Mozart quintets as well, while recognizing that he was not 'into' music as he had been in previous years.[34]

His notes and comments on nature were beautifully written and showed a deep enjoyment of his own personal engagement with God's creation around him. For example, he wrote: 'The morning was dark, with a harder bluer darkness than yesterday. The hills stood out stark and black, the pines were black over thin pale sheets of snow. A more interesting and tougher murki-ness.'[35] The change of seasons and the snow captivated him, and his responses were those of an expectant child living a new and exciting experience, in comments such as 'it is turning into the most brilliant of winters'.[36]

Merton never spoke about his own practice of prayer or of his relationship with God, but he made an exception in his correspondence with Abdul Aziz, who received long and detailed descriptions of Merton's way of prayer and his understanding of God. The rubric of this correspondence outlines Merton's privacy regarding his own prayer movements when he warned Abdul Aziz, saying: 'I do not ordinarily write about such things and ask you therefore to be discreet about it.'[37] Merton's description of his prayer was simple and direct, and he wrote: 'It is centred entirely on attention to the presence of God and to His will and His love. That is to say that it is centred on *faith* by which alone we can know the presence of God.'[38]

A philosophy of solitude

The historical and biographical aspects of Merton's life as a hermit have been outlined in his diaries and his letters; however, those writings contained little of what Merton thought about his time alone, his own reflection on the aspects of solitude that constituted a Christian charisma and the centrality of solitude in the search for a purposeful desert.[39] It is possible to argue that solitude can be sought for personal gain. This gain can have many aspects, such as the gain of tranquillity, independence from others or a personal self-fulfilment in doing whatever one always wanted to do without explaining it to others. In the case of Merton his search for the monastic life, for the eremitic life within a monastery and his search for personal solitude responded to his own search for a closer and fuller encounter with God.

Merton wrote about solitude in his 30-page essay 'Notes for a philosophy of solitude' (1960), in which he elaborated previous arguments that had defended monasticism and eremitism.[40] The important and crucial contribution of the 'Notes' lies in the fact that he extended his thoughts and reflections on solitude to lay people. The three main sections, 'The tyranny of diversion', 'In the sea of perils' and 'Spiritual poverty' clearly located monasticism and solitude within a larger Christian vocation, and thoughts of solitude with God as part of the charisma of the universal Church and not solely of a chosen few.

In the section on 'The tyranny of diversion', Merton argues that every human being is a solitary in the existential sense and that if this has not been realized in personal awareness it is because noises and activities of the world have impeded that self-realization of being, of self, of solitude. Among those diversions there are central activities that numb the solitary, such as the amassing of money in order to acquire status, and the justification of one's own existence without remembering the existence of others within the human race. People who live with those diversions are not alienated from the world as they fit well into society, but the diversions impede them from appreciating their true worth as persons in solitude. Thus, every human being is a distinct person in solitude and not a single part of a larger community structure. Once the diversions disappear there is a confusion rather than personal assertion, but it is through this process of confusion that God appears and helps restore the self-awareness of one's solitude within a larger, busy and noisy world. This confusion requires faith in order to accept God's action and, in my view, differentiates Merton's idea of solitude from any other process of enlightenment or self-discovery.

This model and understanding of solitude was proposed for everybody within the Church and it was published in advance of the reforms proposed by the Second Vatican Council that were to bring a significant change in the understanding of Church. In the second section, 'In the sea of perils', Merton outlines the fact that the solitary is not fleeing society but transcending it, bringing new values that make society as it was obsolete. The solitary renounces everything that does not transcend and as a result renounces the short-lived illusions of diversion. However, the solitary does not live a personal dream of individualism but a challenge to the diversions offered by a society in which the transcendent does not have a place.

For Merton, the individualist world is not the desert but the womb. For the solitary, the loneliness that takes place is not the loneliness of the individual but the loneliness of God. The hermit then is for Merton a witness, a silent witness to a profound truth: the presence of God. Contemplation for a hermit does not become an esoteric exercise or realization but an awareness of the presence of God, in sympathy with others, that becomes a profound act of love, filled with the love of God. There is a clear difference here from the metaphysics of cognition in Christian spirituality that borrows from Greek thought; instead, Merton dwells on and develops a way of contemplation and solitude that later would lead him into a presence of emptiness. Thus, Merton connected with the Christian mystics of the West as well as with the contemplative schools of the East symbolized through his study of Zen contemplation and emptiness.[41]

For Merton, contemplation and the act of solitude is an action because it expresses love and points towards the source of love: God. The contemplative and the solitary withdraw from the world not in order to escape the world but to heal it, through an act of love and communication with God that takes into solitude the world as it is, in need of transcendence and in need of love.

A further characteristic of Merton's treatise on solitude is that for him the perfect solitude is not always expressed by the institutional life of the Carthusians or the Camaldolese but by those who have been chosen by solitude and who through the hard way have been drawn by solitude to experience the love of God in that solitude. Those who are chosen by solitude experience disillusionment and hardship and become true solitaries with God because they have lost completely the illusion that the world is trying to give them and have found themselves solely in God.

One has to ask if Merton was speaking about his own situation as monk and contemplative at the Abbey of Gethsemani.

Merton's description of the true hermit in the second part of the essay refers to a harsh experience of spirituality in that a hermit becomes a metaphor and an example of all Christians because the hermit's encounter with God is the necessary experience of all Christians who at one point or another need to confront God face to face and alone. For Merton asserts over and again that the coenobitic life, that life in community that is lived by the Cistercians, is a proclamation of death to the values of the world but contradicts the life of a solitary hermit, who in poverty and humility leaves concerns for community safety and shows sympathy to other human beings while confronting God alone, following every moment of silence as a path to God.

Thus, in part three of his 'Notes' and within a section on 'Spiritual poverty', Merton introduces the characteristics of the solitary as a person searching for solitude with God but with the frustrations and insecurities of every human being. The solitary life is God's will even when others have not reached this realization. For the solitary life speaks of 'a common humanity' in which all are solitary and in need of God, a solitude that leads to 'compassion' and to a final break of distinctions of what belongs to one person or another. In these thoughts in part three of his 'Notes' and within the use of the terms 'a common humanity' and 'compassion', one can see the seeds of commonality with the spirituality and tenets of Tibetan Buddhism. Those common ideas on contemplation and solitude were to create rapport between Merton and the Fourteenth Dalai Lama in their encounter in India at the end of 1968.[42]

Merton outlined the difference between an 'I' of individualism that can be cultivated and the 'I' of the spirit that can only be and act. The solitary 'I' of the spirit comes from God because it is through this 'I' that a human being encounters God who is another solitary 'I'. The gift of solitude is a gift of the spirit and the sacramental manifestation of the encounter between a solitary soul and God is Christ himself, God manifested and incarnated.

Contemplation as life

What becomes very clear while reading Merton's writings about solitude and contemplation is that, despite his volatile comments related to life in Gethsemani, he was a contemplative at heart, and that contemplation and prayer drove his daily life. Despite the fact that he had many visitors, he was very clear that proposed meetings were not to take place in the hermitage. Thus, in a letter of October 1967 regarding the possibility of giving some conferences to lay people from Louisville, organized by the local bishop, Merton summarized his feelings as follows:

> I have got beyond the stage where I think these conferences can really fit into my life: if it had been ten years ago I might have undertaken more, but now I am used to solitude and have a great deal of work of my own that is not getting done, so that when I do have to get mixed up in several days of visits, it is a real disruption.[43]

Nevertheless, he gave talks to some visitors to the abbey who also visited the hermitage, and in December 1967 preached a retreat to a group of 15 contemplative nuns who gave Merton new positive insights into the contemplative life and the religious communities living the Christian charisma of contemplation.[44] He celebrated Mass for them at the hermitage and they ended singing the song, 'We shall overcome', with a sense of a contemplative revolution on its way.[45]

And he continued expanding his thought on the 'barbarity of the Viet Nam War'.[46] Merton was immensely worried about the US declaration of war on North Korea, expressing his belief that the US Government was preparing the scenario for another world war.[47] Together with his preoccupation for Vietnam he also despaired about the ongoing unjust treatment of blacks within the USA.[48]

It is difficult to understand what follows in Merton's life during 1967–8: a hermit who wanted solitude started travelling all over the USA and Asia as only Merton could do it, at speed. In the words of Lawrence Cunningham:

> Merton got the opportunity to travel and he did so at such pace that were we simply to map out his various comings and goings in the United States and Asia it would require a chapter in its own right.[49]

The fact is that by the end of summer 1968 Merton travelled to Asia after several weeks in California, always searching for new locations for a quieter monastic life. If he had the thought of being a hermit away from Gethsemani or in another place this would remain a mystery; however, it is a fact that the hermit searching for quiet and solitude did absolutely the opposite, a sign of the freedom and creative spirituality of Merton the hermit and Merton the writer.

It is possible to argue that Merton would have liked to stay as a hermit in Asia, at least for a while, to learn more about the East, but the only ones who had formally requested his transfer from Gethsemani were the Trappists in Latin America. In 1967 Brother Frederic Collins wrote to Merton from the newly acquired foundation in Chile, asking him if he would move to Chile if members of the community were to elect him as prior. Merton sent a negative reply but added that he would consider helping for a short time in Chile.[50] By December, Merton thought that it was possible that he would have to go to Chile, and mentioned in his diary that Br Frederic and Fr Callistus, two Trappists living at the Chilean foundation, were going to be at Gethsemani soon for the election of the new abbot.[51] By January he was set on rejecting any election to be prior in Chile or even to go there for a temporary appointment.[52] It was Latin America that had attracted him over the years, the subject of the next chapter.

5

Merton and Latin America

———•◦•———

It can be argued that Merton connected his own understanding of contemplation, the public sphere and the political spheres to two geographical areas outside the USA: Latin America and Asia. If Latin America was the place to which he wanted to escape in order to relive the spirit of monasticism, it was in Asia that he found a home and his passage from this life to the next, the subject of the next chapter.

Merton never visited Latin America, but before becoming a hermit his wish was to live there; at the time when monks from the Abbey of Gethsemani went to Chile to take over a foundation, he was hoping to be selected as one of the party. In the end, the monks departed in September 1966 at the very time that he was making his commitment to remain a hermit at Gethsemani, convinced that after all his health would not have allowed him to depart and settle in a monastic foundation in Latin America.[1] In a way, what drove Merton was the construction of an image in which he perceived Latin America as a paradise and Latin American writers as courageous and creative people.

This chapter explores Merton's connections with Latin America and the influences he had on Ernesto Cardenal and the monastic community of Solentiname (Nicaragua) as well as the influences that Latin American writers such as Nicanor Parra had in Merton's own life, daily contemplation and writing. This is an area of Merton's life that Malgorzata Poks has recently explored, arguing that 'the absence of any sustained effort to analyze the Latin American connection in his life and work seems all the more intriguing'.[2] She provides a full study of Merton's engagement with Latin Americans, following Robert Daggy's lead, who in 1991 had argued that Merton wrote 'to and for Latin Americans'.[3] Among those Latin Americans the Nicaraguan, Ernesto Cardenal, occupied a central place in Merton's search for the utopian Latin America and for his dreams of leaving Gethsemani, and the Chilean poet, Nicanor Parra, influenced not only Merton's poetry but also was present on one of those occasions (May 1966) on which the infatuated Merton brought M (Mott calls her S), the nurse he had fallen in love with, to lunch with Parra in Louisville, Kentucky.[4] Cardenal and Parra shared with Merton the fact that they had studied in the USA and therefore were the most likely partners for exchanges on poetry, contemplation and life. They were Latin American writers who could converse with Merton's despair about US society and they were politically against the role of the USA as empire, something else that Merton had in common with them.

Openings through Ernesto Cardenal

Merton's years as a novice master allowed him to come in contact with devout novices from many different countries, including Ernesto Cardenal, the Nicaraguan poet and later a member of the Sandinista Government, who was at Gethsemani for two years but was advised to leave because of ill health,[5] as stated in Chapter 1. Cardenal was born in Granada, Nicaragua, on 20 January 1925, son of Rodolfo and Esmeralda (Martínez) Cardenal, within one of the first Spanish families to have arrived from Europe in the twentieth century.[6] When he was five years old they moved to the town of León, where Rubén Darío, the greatest Nicaraguan poet, had been born. Cardenal was educated in a Catholic school run by the Christian Brothers until he was ten years of age, when his parents sent him to the Jesuit boarding school, Centroamérica, in Granada. The school had close contact with two renowned poets, José Coronel Urtecho and Pablo Antonio Cuadra. Cardenal was related to both these poets, and his grandmother encouraged him to read poetry at all times. At the school the Spanish Jesuit and poet, Angel Martínez Baigorri, also guided him and encouraged him to write poetry. It is said that his love for a young lady, Carmen, triggered a vast number of his early poems; however, the main influences on his early poetry were Pablo Neruda and César Vallejo.[7]

After completing secondary school, Cardenal studied philosophy and literature at universities in Mexico (1942–6) and English literature at Columbia University, USA (1947–9). It was in New York that Cardenal was influenced by Ezra Pound and where he read the poems of Thomas Merton for the first time.[8] It was by reading and studying US poetry and Pound's plain treatment of his subject, without using any superfluous words, that Cardenal found his own vein of direct and revolutionary poetry.[9] It was by reading Merton and by his own life with Merton that Cardenal made poverty a sine qua non for the act of poetry and the life of a poet.

After a few months in Madrid and Paris, in 1950 he returned to Nicaragua and became an active member of the revolutionary group, the National Union for Popular Action (UNAP). In 1952 he had to go into hiding because of his political activities, and he took part in the failed plot against Somoza in 1954. UNAP had planned to surprise Somoza inside his palace and take power. The plan collapsed because there were not enough plotters, and most of them were arrested after one of Cardenal's comrades, under torture, gave away all the information needed by the security forces. Cardenal's hiding is mentioned in his poem 'Hora 0'.[10]

In 1956, when the poet Rigoberto López Pérez assassinated President Somoza, Cardenal underwent a religious conversion and applied to become a Trappist monk in the USA. He entered the Trappist Abbey of Gethsemani in Kentucky on 8 May 1957 and started his novitiate on 14 May, when Thomas Merton was the novice master.[11] Cardenal had to sign an agreement with the abbot, stating that he would not write poetry or at least would not have it published, and he took a new name, Mary Lawrence.[12] His love for God and the renunciation of the life he loved made him join the austerity of Gethsemani, thus rejecting the possibility of being a priest in Nicaragua and also rejecting any further enjoyment of the natural beauty and lakes of Nicaragua, sites that he loved very much.[13] In his memoirs, Cardenal recalls how, when he arrived at the US immigration entry port, the customs officer reminded him that the only way he could be admitted to the USA was by immigrating for life, and he welcomed him to a new country, a new life and a commitment to live in Gethsemani for the rest of his life.[14]

During his first days at Gethsemani, Cardenal had a mentor who guided him and taught him among other things a sign language, totally silent, that had been developed by the Trappists during the twelfth century.[15] The sign language was useful because the life of the Trappists was lived in complete silence and even the sign language could not be used between 7.00 p.m. and 7.00 a.m., the period of the Grand Silence. Cardenal remembers that the novices didn't join the community for morning office or Mass but had Mass with Merton who, later in the day, would work, sowing tomato seeds, for example, together with the novices. During daily life there were no breaks between prayer, study, manual work and meals, so that for Cardenal that life was 'a life of love' without holidays.[16] Monks didn't have personal watches but there were big clocks all over the abbey; indeed there was an infirmary and all the necessities for life, such as cooks and barbers.[17]

Shortly after his arrival, Merton mentioned to Cardenal the possibility of a monastic Trappist foundation from Gethsemani in Nicaragua, and over the following decade both of them would write to each other about the possibilities.[18] However, Merton, who wanted to move to Latin America, was never allowed to join the Trappists who took over a foundation in Santiago, Chile. Even the abbot was learning Spanish in case they needed him in Latin America as the monasteries in the USA were being filled very quickly and at that time there were almost a thousand Trappist monks in the USA. Because of that possible foundation and Cardenal's literary past, Merton asked him to check the Spanish translation of *The Seven Storey Mountain* that had been commissioned by Editorial Sudamericana.[19] Merton also was honest with Cardenal about his criticisms towards what he started to call the 'Trappist Corporation', comments that unsettled Cardenal, who was very happy at Gethsemani and wanted to continue growing in his practice of the monastic life.[20]

Parts of Cardenal's memoirs were filled with the daily community meeting, the chapter, in which deceased Trappists were remembered and where a monk read a chapter of the *Rule of St Benedict*.[21] During the chapter of faults, in which monks asked pardon from the community for their trespasses, one monk was singled out by the abbot and had to confess a particular fault; in the case of Cardenal he always asked pardon for being late, while he was accused by others of being noisy when closing doors and of speaking loudly to a visitor (Pablo Antonio Cuadra).[22] At that time there were almost 200 people in Gethsemani, and it was a very large community that gathered to listen to the rule and to encourage each other to continue the life of John the Baptist in the desert, as Merton used to tell the novices.

One of the problems faced by Cardenal was his inability to sing and to chant the office in chapel. Despite having several teachers, he was unable to appreciate the different tones, and Merton told him that such lack of a musical ear was an impediment for priestly ordination because the priest needed to lead the singing during the High Mass.[23] However, the abbot thought that this would not be a problem as within the new Latin American foundation there would probably be other liturgical

ways. It was during this discussion that Cardenal expressed his
opinion that his call was to a contemplative life rather than to
the Catholic priesthood and that he would be happy to remain
as a non-ordained Trappist within Gethsemani. This personal
identity was very important at that moment because it would
give meaning to all Cardenal's life, where contemplation took
precedence over the priesthood and over his ministerial duties
in government, so much so that when Cardenal had to attend
musical events he immersed himself in prayer as he wasn't able
to discern the quality of the music being played in front of him
as minister of culture in the Sandinista Government.

It was Merton who introduced Cardenal to the value of the
indigenous thought and spirituality of North and South America,
and Merton always insisted that the Latin American monastery
to be opened should have indigenous monks as well as those
from North America. The impact was enormous in Cardenal's
poetry and writing in general as the indigenous and the pre-
Colombian peoples and myths started filling his poetry after
he left Gethsemani.[24]

Cardenal had a constant headache and stomach ache during
his last few months in Gethsemani. The monk-doctor diagnosed
that the gastritis was caused by nervous tension, which created
the headaches, because Cardenal recognized that once the bell
for the office in chapel rang, he started feeling ill. The doctor
suggested that the problem would be solved only by Cardenal's
leaving Gethsemani and joining another, less strict contemplative community such as the Benedictines.[25] It was decided that
Cardenal should leave Gethsemani, and once the decision was
taken Merton introduced him to Dom Gregorio Lemercier, prior
of the Benedictine monastery in Cuernavaca (Mexico), who
welcomed him.[26]

Thus, at the end of July 1959 Cardenal left Gethsemani with
Merton's clear instructions to wait for him in Cuernavaca as
Merton was applying to leave Gethsemani.[27] When Cardenal
met Merton for the last time before he left, he knelt in front

of Merton requesting his blessing. Years later, in October 1965, when Cardenal was already a priest and visited Merton in order to discuss the new contemplative community in Solentiname, Merton knelt in front of Cardenal in order to receive his blessing.[28]

Contemplative life in Solentiname

From Gethsemani, Cardenal went to Mexico City and then to Cuernavaca, where he conveyed messages from Merton to Lemercier regarding Merton's request to leave Gethsemani. Merton's request needed to be assessed by his spiritual director; the later-to-be Cardinal of Paris, Jean Daniélou, who could not agree with Merton's changing his vow of stability as a Trappist for another experimental way of contemplative life.[29] However, neither Cardenal nor Merton knew this at that time, and Cardenal proceeded to follow Merton's instructions on arriving at the monastery in Cuernavaca as a guest. The Benedictine monastery, Santa María de la Resurrección of Cuernavaca, was ahead of its time; at the time of Cardenal's arrival the liturgy was already being sung in Spanish rather than Latin, and the church was filled with beautiful contemporary icons. The Belgian Lemercier put a heavy emphasis on psychoanalytical techniques and group therapy related to the religious life and contemplation and, years later in 1962, the Vatican ordered him not to use those techniques any longer; as a result Lemercier left the religious life and got married, a fact that made Merton very sad because a new way of being contemplative tried in Cuernavaca had been lost forever.[30]

Cardenal was 34 years old in 1959, and his two first books had just been published with the titles *Epigramas* and *Hora 0*. He had been a guest at the monastery for only a short time and he continued corresponding with Merton, who was still hopeful that he would leave Gethsemani and arrive in Cuernavaca.[31] Merton's abbot was suspicious; the letters were marked 'conscience matter', indicating absolute privacy from the abbot's censorship. However, at the end of the year Merton wrote to Dom Lemercier and to Cardenal, informing them that he had received a letter from Rome rejecting his request to leave Gethsemani and that he was not to pursue this matter any longer.[32] At the same time Merton offered to continue as novice master because he would then have the opportunity to have some personal solitude and he was 'better off here than at any other time in the monastery'.[33] Further, Merton supported Cardenal's efforts in Nicaragua and accepted the will of the Sacred Congregation as God's will for him.[34] Merton seemed to move on very quickly and he requested Jean Daniélou to continue offering him spiritual counsel.[35]

After his ordination, Cardenal was not sent to a parish but started a priestly life that was to be rather different from that of other priests. Merton had talked to Cardenal about the possibility of opening a branch of Gethsemani in Nicaragua, and Cardenal continued to be enchanted with the idea of a simple and contemplative life closer to the original life of the Trappists.[36] As Merton could not join him, while he had the intention of doing so, Cardenal moved to the islands of Solentiname together with two former Colombian classmates, Carlos Alberto and William Agudelo.[37] Two poets, Pablo Antonio Cuadra and José Coronel Urtecho, accompanied them on their journey.[38] Three of them started their community life on 13 February 1966 but the Colombians did not last. Merton, who was closely informed about Cardenal's foundation, recognized in a letter to Ludovico Silva that Cardenal's task was not easy, writing that 'you have no idea how difficult and complex a task he has taken upon himself, to be a poet and a priest at the same time and in a society that is completely fed up with priests'.[39]

Carlos Alberto found that a monastic life did not suit him, while William Agudelo missed his Colombian girlfriend, Teresita. They both left but eventually Agudelo and Teresita rejoined the monastic community that, after consultation with Merton, had been expanded to allow married people. The monastic community followed the traditional search for God through the recognition that contemplation led to him. It is interesting that Cardenal recognized that, although he went to Solentiname searching for God in contemplation, he found a God who eventually led him to others, to revolution and to Marxism as a tool for social change. It was the reading of the Gospels that led him to Marxism; it was contemplation that led him to revolution.[40]

Cardenal identified his community with a lay monastery under the name of Our Lady of Solentiname. William Agudelo and Teresita had two children, named Irene and Juan, and they were joined by some local young men, Alejandro, Elbis and Laureano. They lived on the products of the land. While from the start they cultivated the land, they were forced also to work on the production of objects that could be sold and indeed were later sold all over the world. These included ashtrays, candlesticks and souvenirs in the shape of local fauna. They shared their profits in a common purse and supplied the needs of each individual community member. The utopian nature of the community was summarized by Cardenal's wish that one day there would be no money in the world and that everybody would be filled with love for each other.

When the monastic experiment ended, because of the bombardment of the islands by the armed forces of Somoza, some of the transcripts of the conversations that had taken place after the reading of the Gospel at the Sunday Mass in Solentiname became important testimonies to Cardenal's creativity and to the driving force of contemplation in the life of a priest who by then had become identified with the politics of the Nicaraguan revolution and with the involvement of Latin American priests in politics. However, as Cardenal expressed it during the moments in which he found the life of a government minister tough, he was interrupting his contemplative life only in order to serve the people; he was looking forward to the day when he would cease to be a politician.

In the two volumes of *The Gospel in Solentiname*, Cardenal explains through a short introduction the *Sitz im Leben* of the commentaries collated and published in Europe.[41] Cardenal stresses the fact that there were different personalities involved in the commentaries that, in the end, were the work of the Spirit in an archipelago in which not everybody had access to a boat to reach Cardenal's community, and within a eucharistic celebration during which copies of the New Testament were distributed to all participants, some of whom, and particularly the elderly, could not read the text.[42] After the Mass all participants shared a simple but communal lunch.

Cardenal the poet and the politician, I would argue, is a product of Cardenal the contemplative who, in contemplating God's work in the world and in society, remains as enamoured with God as he was at the time of his departure for Gethsemani. His 'exteriorist' poetry, as Cardenal described his poetry in the 1950s, became more and more cosmical, political and personal, linking his own contemplative life with his role as government minister.[43] Cardenal wrote to Merton until 1968, sharing some of those ideas on contemplation and politics that were to germinate later in the community at Solentiname and in the years of service by Cardenal to the Nicaraguan revolution.

The influence of anti-poetry

Merton's literary excellence meant that he kept a group of literary friends with whom he corresponded extensively and who recognized Merton as a writer. For Merton, this division of roles was artificial as all his literary writings, including poems, came out of his monastic experience and his personal contemplative life. He corresponded with Evelyn Waugh, Jacques Maritain, the Chilean poet Nicanor Parra, the Venezuelan poet Ludovico Silva and the Argentinian writer Victoria Ocampo.[44] Merton's interest in Latin America and its writers remained one of his most interesting traits because, unlike other friends,

Merton shared with them literary pieces rather than faith or religion.

In the case of Nicanor Parra, for example, the Chilean poet was an atheist and member of one of the most prominent Communist families of Chile; however, unlike his relatives Nicanor Parra didn't follow an artistic career but a university one, having studied mathematics, physics and cosmology at Brown University and the University of Oxford, becoming later a professor of theoretical physics at the Chilean University in Santiago. As with most Chilean poets, writing poetry was a pastime and his income came from his university position. Together with James Laughlin, Parra visited Merton in May 1966 and Merton wrote to him beforehand, exchanging poems and suggestions. During that year Parra was visiting professor at the University of Louisiana (Baton Rouge) and read his poetry at the international meeting of the PEN Club in New York. Other poetry recitals took place at Berkeley, Los Angeles and other universities in California. After their meeting, Merton wrote a warm letter to Parra on the occasion of Parra's sister's death (by suicide) with the following words: 'I am very sorry, and wish I could say something that might help you in your sorrow. But there are occasions when words are no help. In my friendship I think of you and share your sorrow.'[45]

Parra became well known in international circles for the publication in 1954 of his so-called 'anti-poetry', published within a collection of poetry and anti-poetry in which Parra refused to create aesthetic categories removed from reality and shaped poetry not as metaphor but as ordinary, daily, contemporary reality itself.[46] For example, in his poem, 'The Pilgrim', he writes:

> I see a bridge
> and a car that disappears among the buildings.[47]

In 1969 Parra was awarded the Chilean National Prize of Literature for *Poemas & Antipoemas* and became more and more a recluse in his seaside home of Las Cruces. Merton was very conscious of Parra's realism within poetry. A man of the 1938 Chilean generation of writers, Parra did not share Merton's faith in God but he shared poetry as the contemplation of the daily life of all. Merton commented in his letters on the monastic and contemplative quality of Parra's poetry and outlook. Thus, in 1965, after reading Parra's poetry collection *Versos de Salón*, a book that Parra had posted to him, Merton remarked that 'I agree with your dissonances, and find them to be in fact very monastic', following with Merton's criticism of monastic life and monks as happily following 'a square society'.[48]

Part of the fascination of Merton for writers in general and Latin American writers in particular came from his sense that 'today the poets and artists tend to fulfil many of the functions that were once the monopoly of monks'.[49] This comment speaks clearly of the utopian vision that Merton had about Latin American writers. However, it is possible to argue that Merton and Parra shared a common characteristic, that is, their individual positioning against a world they sometimes challenged and even despised. Merton overemphasized this, I hope, when he described his contemporary time to Parra as 'a time of the worst barbarity, much worse than in the time of the fall of the Roman empire'.[50] Merton wanted desperately to be a hermit; Parra wanted all his life to be left on his own and departed for a quiet seaside resort where journalists found it extremely difficult to get him to give interviews or to become a media product.

Merton and Parra had a meeting of minds and souls at a time when both of them were challenging poetry as an aesthetic category of shared hermeneutical invention. Poks has correctly remarked that 'for at least a decade prior to his death, Merton had been concerned with the necessity of creating anti-art as a challenge to the dominant art-cult that reduced artistic production to mere self-expression and self-advertisement'.[51] Thus, Merton found a fellow culprit and companion in his own aesthetic crime of talking poetically about reality, something that Parra had mastered well. Parra had been consistent within his own poetic project, understood by the Mertonian scholar, Paul Pearson, as 'to strip away the superficial trimmings of poetry, its poetic language, and to present language heard in its reality'.[52]

Merton simply stated his strong opinion: 'I think it is important to write antipoems like Parra.'[53] According to Poks, Merton's first attempt at writing anti-poetry was the poem, 'Original Child Bomb' (1962), 'a prose meditation on the construction and explosion of the first atomic bomb, known as Little Boy'.[54] Later, the 88 sections of Merton's *Cables to the Ace* (1968) was to give a poetic narrative to his own sense of an anti-culture that was far from the ordinary values of daily anti-poetry.[55]

Already in 1965 Merton had spoken of Parra as a 'wonderful poet'.[56] By early 1966 he wrote to Ludovico Silva about his liking for Parra's poetry.[57] Merton wrote several times to Parra and mentioned to others that Parra was 'an important poet', requesting information about Parra's participation in the congress of poets in La Habana.[58] Their meeting in May 1966 took place at Gethsemani when James Laughlin of New Directions – Merton's editor and also Parra's North American editor – brought the Chilean poet to the abbey.[59] The meeting was friendly and warm but, of course, included Merton's attention to his friend, nurse M, something that amused Parra who probably was not embarrassed but felt close to the human self of Thomas Merton. Writing to Cardenal, Merton described the visit as a 'good visit'.[60] In April 1967, Merton wrote to Parra in no uncertain terms saying 'Keep well, write more poems, come back.'[61]

The untimely death of Merton in Asia prevented further correspondence and cooperation with poets and writers from Latin America, but there is no doubt that Merton had a certain way of cultivating their friendship and he was successful at translating some of their poems into English.[62] However, by 1967

Merton was fully immersed in the search for a fuller contemplation that for him came from the East. Thus, once there was an opportunity to visit Asia he pursued this opportunity vigorously and, during early 1968, had less correspondence with Latin American writers. His trip to Asia dominated his concerns in what was to be the last journey of his biological life, the subject of the next chapter.

6

Merton's final trip to Asia

---◆·◆·◆---

It was very fitting that the Cistercian hermit who had met so many and had corresponded with countless people about the problems and anxieties of his 1960s contemporary world would decide to ask for permission to accept an invitation to go to Asia. Changes in his own life after three years in the hermitage meant that during 1968 Merton spent some time giving talks, retreats and visiting New Mexico, Alaska and California. These journeys were triggered by the election of a new abbot, Dom Flavian Burns OCSO on 15 January 1968.[1]

Dom Flavian entered the Abbey of Gethsemani in 1951, aged 19, and became one of the youngest abbots after his election at the age of 36. Dom Flavian had accepted election with the condition that after five years he would return to life as a hermit, and so he did after having to deal with Merton's departure for Asia and his unexpected return to the abbey's cemetery. To become an abbot after the Second Vatican Council in 1968 was tricky and challenging with all the reforms expected by the Council, but to be an abbot in an abbey where Fr Louis (Thomas Merton) was a resident hermit was even trickier. But relations between them were good. Dom Flavian had been one of Merton's scholastics in the 1950s and they used to meet regularly when they were both hermits. In the words of Michael Casagram OCSO:

> Fr. Flavian . . . played a crucial role in the history of Gethsemani, being the abbot who really initiated us into the changes of Vatican II, though these were well on the way when he became abbot in 1968.[2]

It was all fitting and much related to the spirit of the Second Vatican Council that Dom Flavian allowed Merton to go and search for further ways in which to make Gethsemani a place of more prayer and solitude by meeting other leaders of contemplative communities that followed the *Rule of St Benedict* in Asia.[3]

Part of this trip was also triggered by the mandate to Merton from Dom Flavian to search for places where Merton himself could find a place to live his hermit life once he returned from Asia. Dom Flavian's opinion was that Gethsemani had become a busy place with many visitors and a crowded place with many monks, and that eventually hermits would have to search for quiet monasteries in California or Arizona and even in Asia. It must be remembered that Dom Flavian was a hermit for most of his life, and while he served several terms as abbot in three different abbeys (Gethsemani in Kentucky, Holy Cross Abbey in Virginia and Assumption Abbey in Missouri), these were periods of monastic service in which he interrupted his continuous life as a hermit; to be a hermit within the Cistercian tradition was his vocation.[4]

Within the climate of more openness and less fear of encountering the world, Merton struggled with many invitations to give lectures and retreats but was encouraged by his new abbot to attend a meeting in Bangkok in which members of different Asian monastic communities were discussing the renewal and a much-needed reaffirmation of Christian monastic communities in Asia. Merton was certainly very pleased about this and spoke warmly about the opportunity to Brother Patrick Hart, who was to become his secretary and dealt with his correspondence and manuscripts while he was away from the abbey.[5]

The invitation and the meeting outlined the post-Second Vatican Council openness to the world religions and particularly to the Buddhist monastic experience, for in the area of interfaith dialogue and relations with other world religions the

Second Vatican Council had produced a very forward-looking declaration, stating that:

> The Catholic Church rejects nothing of what is true and holy in these religions. She has a high regard for the manner of life and conduct, the precepts and doctrines which, although differing in many ways from her own teaching, nevertheless often reflect a ray of that truth which enlightens all men.[6]

The Second Vatican Council also made a particularly positive description of Buddhism in the same document and with the following terms:

> Buddhism in its various forms testifies to the essential inadequacy of this changing world. It proposes a way of life by which men can, with confidence and trust, attain a state of perfect liberation and reach supreme illumination either through their own efforts or by the aid of divine help.[7]

Merton's trip to Asia became, in the spirit of the Council, a journey of love in which one of the most prominent Catholics in the USA journeyed to the only continent where Christianity was and still is a minority, in order to learn about the joys and hopes of religious practitioners within Asia and to engage himself in dialogue with the strangers of the past, fellow pilgrims and fellow human beings of the present and the future. Merton assumed the challenges of the modern world, stating very clearly that 'It is the peculiar office of the monk in the modern world to keep alive the contemplative experience and to keep the way open for modern technological man to recover the integrity of his own inner depths.'[8]

This chapter examines the pilgrim experience of a Christian monk encountering the Buddhist East, in particular his meetings with the Fourteenth Dalai Lama in Dharamsala, India.[9] The chapter highlights: (1) the commonality of the spiritual experience; (2) the difference of context and path; and (3) the common call to kindness and love for the stranger stressed by the Dalai Lama's opening remarks in his Nobel Prize lecture of 1989:

I am always reminded that we are all basically alike: we are all human beings. Maybe we have different clothes, our skin is of a different colour, or we speak different languages. This is on the surface. But basically, we are the same human beings. That is what binds us to each other.[10]

In its conclusions this chapter outlines Merton's contribution to the possibilities of interfaith dialogue between faith communities of the so-called world religions through (1) common contemplation, (2) daily study of other traditions and (3) the common service to strangers.

Merton's Tibetan experience of the stranger

Merton's trip to Asia came about due to an invitation extended by a Benedictine international working group (Aide à l'Implantation Monastique) that was helping the possible implementation of renewal throughout the world as required by the Second Vatican Council. The conference was for Western monasteries to support those in the Global South and the idea was to gather in a conference all Asian monastic leaders, including Benedictine and Cistercian, in Bangkok, Thailand, in December 1968. Merton agreed to give an address to the Spiritual Summit Conference in Calcutta and to give a series of talks at different monasteries in Asia. However, he wanted to visit as many Buddhist monasteries as possible so that, according to his secretary, Brother Patrick Hart, 'Thomas Merton's pilgrimage to Asia was an effort on his part to deepen his own religious and monastic commitment.'[11] Thus, Merton was connecting Christian and Buddhist practices of meditation in order to refresh his contemplation and his subsequent actions of personal and social concern for others in need.

It cannot be overstated that Merton's position was unusual on three counts: dialogue with other Christians, let alone with other world religions, was not the norm in the pre-Second Vatican Council climate of Catholicism; Cistercian monks didn't undertake speaking tours for weeks without end; and the cold war and the Vietnam war created an ever more insular USA. Within this insular development, US citizens were certainly discouraged from visiting Asia, a continent that at that time was been swept by Chinese communists and the influence of the Soviet Union in many emerging socialist-oriented regimes.

However, and despite this international climate of war, Merton had a sustained interest in Asian monasticism and had read extensively on Zen and Buddhism in general.[12] If he had not died in December 1968 it is possible that Merton would have done groundbreaking work in interfaith Christian–Buddhist relations. His Asian trip was also authorized by his abbot so as to report back on the possibilities of Cistercian expansion of monastic communities in Asia; this despite the fact that Merton's abbot had little confidence in the practicality of Merton as a decision-maker. On a previous occasion Merton had explored the possibilities of founding monastic communities in Alaska and, because he visited Alaska during autumn, he had missed the point that during winter the visibility through bad weather, fog and long periods of dark was nil. If the Cistercians had followed Merton's advice to push for a monastic foundation in Alaska, it would have come as quite a surprise to the founding monks that they could not see anything around them during the winter months.

Throughout his visit to Asia, Merton wrote a diary, which was published after his death, in which the leitmotif was his ongoing search for further solitude. It is possible that many who read Merton's diary would ask: 'Why did he go to Asia then, instead of getting on with daily contemplation and monastic solitude?' Further solitude seems to be a common theme in all Merton's writings; despite the apparent contradiction of wanting to maintain contact with a wide variety of people while envisaging the hermit life as the end of the road and something that he wanted.

The journey home

Merton departed from San Francisco to Hawaii on 15 October 1968 and from there travelled to Tokyo, Hong Kong and Bangkok. Merton's first writings during the journey were as usual exhilarating and all-embracing as he wrote: 'I am going home, to the home where I have never been in this body.'[13] On 17 October Merton landed in a humid and hot Bangkok and remarked on the lifeless, powerful officials at the airport.[14] Merton stayed at the Oriental Hotel, a quiet, safe place, and as his first activity took a taxi to Wat Bovoranives (one of the traditional Buddhist temples of Bangkok) and to the home of a writer on Buddhism, Phra Khantipalo, who discussed meditation with Merton and told him that in a few days he was going to the northeast, to a monastery in the forest, where he would have a good meditation teacher.[15] On 18 October Merton was driven to see Phra Pathom Chedi, one of the oldest and largest dome-shaped Buddhist shrines in Thailand.[16]

After two days of new experiences, Merton was driven in the evening of 19 October to Bangkok Airport for his departure for Calcutta, where he stayed until 27 October.[17] Like anybody visiting the big Indian cities for the first time, Merton was overwhelmed by the amount of people, cows, movement and noise; he wrote: 'Calcutta, smiling, fecal, detached, tired, inexhaustible, young-old, full of young people who seem old, is the *unmasked* city.'[18] By 20 October, Merton had settled to reading the great Tibetan poet, Milarepa.[19] Further, by chance he had met Chogyam Trungpa Rimpoche, the Tibetan founder of a Buddhist monastery in Scotland, with whom he had lunch and together with him and his secretary boarded a jeep and went to a market to see the preparations for the feast of Divali.[20] By 24 October, Merton had visited the Narendrapur-Ramakrishna Mission Ashram, a complex place that served as college, agricultural school, poultry farm, school for the blind and orphanage.[21]

On 28 October, Merton flew from Calcutta to New Delhi and stayed at the Grand Hotel Oberoi Karma; Merton remarked on 'cows on the front doorstep, and turbaned Janissaries, and girl students in saris raising money for flood relief'.[22] A few days later, Merton complained that the food was too heavy and that he wanted to sleep.[23] In Delhi, he met with lay Tibetans and with a young couple from the US Embassy, Anthony Quainton, specialist on the policies of the kingdom of Bhutan, and his wife.[24] For the most part, though, he read Tucci's works on the Tibetan mandala, Buddhist and Hindu sacred art in a symbolic circular figure. Mandala is a Sanskrit word that means 'circle', used for teaching and for prayer.[25] Judging by the pages and notations in his diary, Merton was impressed by the mandala forms.[26] As with many other things, Merton saw the possibilities of sacred spaces and studied them intensely, assimilating quite quickly the possible connections between his studies and the possible improvement of contemplation and the deepening of monastic life.

In Delhi, Merton made a point of visiting the Ladakh Buddhi Vihara, a school-monastery that at that time hosted Tibetan refugees who had made the crossing from Tibet into India.[27] Merton was impressed by the place and wrote about Lobsang Phuntsok Lhalungpa, a Tibetan broadcaster who ran a radio and Tibetan programs in Delhi, where Merton's contact with the Fourteenth Dalai Lama, Harold Talbott, was taking Tibetan lessons.[28] An American, Talbott had been a student at Harvard University, had become a Catholic and was now studying Buddhism. He had made contact with Merton at Gethsemani and had been confirmed at the abbey.

At the same place in Delhi Merton met some of the monks, including Lama Geshe Tenpa Gyaltsan, a member of the Gelugpa, the monastic order of the Dalai Lama. There was another monk from another Tibetan monastic order, the Nyingmapa, and when both of them were asked by Merton what was the difference they laughed. Merton had met a prominent Nyingmapa,

Nechiung Rimpoche, formerly abbot of the monastery of Nechung and a *tulku*, which is a person who is recognized as a reincarnation of somebody who has gone far in the process of exiting the *samsara* (wandering through) and attaining enlightenment.[29] Merton had a conversation with them about monastic life and they stressed 'the ideas of discipline and detachment from a life of pleasure and materialism'.[30]

On 30 October, Merton dined together with Talbott as guests of the Canadian High Commissioner, and departed in the train to the Himalayas on 31 October.[31] Talbott was to accompany Merton all the way to Darjeeling, where they were to part on 24 November.[32] On 1 November, Merton and Talbott arrived by train in Pathankot and were driven by jeep to the town of Dharamsala.[33] The road to Dharamsala is tortuous today and it must have been less developed in 1968. However, it is a beautiful ascent into the Himalayas and Dharamsala stands tall as quite a large town at the bottom of the hill where the quarters of the Tibetan Government in exile are located, just below the temple and the residence of the Fourteenth Dalai Lama. Talbott was studying with the Dalai Lama, so he and Merton stayed at the cottage that the Dalai Lama had already assigned to Talbott; Merton enjoyed the silence of the place and the ongoing praying attitudes displayed by Tibetans. The most famous Tibetan around Dharamsala was, of course, the Fourteenth Dalai Lama, and Merton had the great opportunity of meeting him a few times and discussing meditation and philosophy. Merton's visit constituted a change for the Fourteenth Dalai Lama, who at that time had complained that there were many Westerners visiting him in Dharamsala out of curiosity but that it was very difficult to discern their intentions.[34]

Merton and the Fourteenth Dalai Lama

It is striking throughout his diary how conversant with Buddhist and Sanskrit terminology Merton was and how all his conversations related to monastic issues and his search for further solitude. Thus, after days of visiting places and people he could only think that he needed a few days of solitude. Maybe because of this the visit to Dharamsala and to the residence of the Fourteenth Dalai Lama became the highlight of his Asian trip.[35] There in the hills of the Himalayas two men – dedicated to contemplation, daily and intense, and dedicated to challenging injustice and war among human beings as a kind of spiritual politics – met. A Christian and a Buddhist discussed their own daily practices and engagement with the transcendent, with the spiritual, with the other-worldly. The significance for Merton and for the Dalai Lama was profound; the significance for others who have read about this encounter years later has been life-transforming.

Merton and the Dalai Lama met three times during November 1968.[36] The Fourteenth Dalai Lama had fled Tibet (now the Tibet Autonomous Region of China) in March 1959, and had sought political asylum in India, establishing over years his government in exile and a very large Tibetan community with temples and schools at the Himalayan town of Dharamsala in northern India. In 1968 'Little Lhasa', as the town is today known, was still small and the Dalai Lama had not had the publicity and world recognition that he was given after receiving the Nobel Prize for Peace in 1989. The prize was given to him because of 'his consistent opposition to the use of violence and his efforts to seek peaceful solutions, based on tolerance and mutual respect, in order to preserve the historical and cultural heritage of his people'.[37] Indeed, Tibetan Buddhism was less known than today; during the 1960s, Western seekers were more familiar with Zen Buddhism and forms of self-enlightenment rather than the possibilities of enlightenment for all sentient beings through personal meditation, as is the aim of Tibetan Buddhism.

The meetings took place at the Dalai Lama's residence in McLeod Ganj, a small Himalayan enclave located in the hills above Dharamsala, described by Merton as 'admirably situated, high over the valley, with snow-covered mountains behind, all pine trees, with apes in them, and a vast view over the plains to the south'.[38] On the day before the first visit, Tenzin Geshe, the Dalai Lama's young secretary, came to arrange time and protocol with Merton.[39] However, if Tenzin was young one must remember that the Fourteenth Dalai Lama was only 33 years old himself at that time.

Merton and Talbott walked up the hill to the Tibetan village, where they were met by Sonam Kazi, who had expected them to arrive by bus. They passed through the empty buildings of Swarg Ashram, where the headquarters of the Dalai Lama had been located previously. Further up they reached a house surrounded by Tibetan prayer flags, the living quarters of the Dalai Lama. They greeted the Dalai Lama's private chaplain, the Khempo of Namgyal Tra-Tsang, who spoke to Merton in his room where he was studying Buddhist texts. Merton tried to discuss metaphysics and the response he got was quite self-explanatory when the Khempo said that:

> the real ground of his Gelugpa study and practice was the knowledge of suffering, and that only when a person was fully convinced of the immensity of suffering and its complete universality and saw the need of deliverance for *all* beings, could he begin to understand sunyata.[40]

Sunyata, emptiness in Sanskrit, embodies the entire meaning of the path to enlightenment and unity with other human beings. This conversation was probably so important for Merton that he transcribed the whole sense of it in his diary, including the Khempo's description of meditation: 'laying the axe to the root'.[41]

Following his visit, Merton suggested to the Dalai Lama's secretary that they should read the weekly edition of *Le Monde* rather than depend on magazines such as *Life*, *Time* and *Reader's Digest*.[42] In Merton's opinion, *Le Monde* was essential and he promised to ask his friend 'Ping' Ferry to put them on his mailing list for the Center for the Study of Democratic Institutions.[43]

For the first meeting between Merton and the Fourteenth Dalai Lama, on 4 November 1968, the Dalai Lama's secretary sent a jeep to collect Merton and Talbott. Their passports were checked by an Indian official at the gates of the Dalai Lama's compound and then Merton was at the new building waiting to be called in. While Merton waited, he noticed that there were shelves with Buddhist works presented to the Dalai Lama by his friend D. T. Suzuki.[44] Merton's description of the Dalai Lama suggests that he had not seen photos or descriptions of him before, as he wrote in his diary:

> The Dalai Lama is most impressive as a person. He is strong and alert, bigger than I expected (for some reason I thought he would be small). A very solid, energetic, generous, and warm, person very capably trying to handle enormous problems – none of which he mentioned directly.[45]

Their first meeting dealt with religion, philosophy and ways of meditating, and Merton listened attentively to the importance of Tibetan Buddhism sometimes criticized by other more traditional Buddhist schools of thought and practice.[46] Merton's knowledge of Tibetan Buddhism must have been good because they discussed *dzogchen*, the 'great perfection', the great way of all-inclusiveness, the esoteric tradition of the Nyingmapas order of Tibetan Buddhism, a tradition that goes back to the eighth century, when great teachers such as Guru Padma Sambhava (Swat Valley) and Vimalamitra (India) visited Tibet. *Dzogchen* constitutes a very direct way to knowledge, and the Dalai Lama told Merton 'not to misunderstand the simplicity of *dzogchen*'.[47] He mentioned to Merton two scholars of Tibetan Buddhism who could help, namely Geshe Sopa of the New Jersey Monastery, who had been teaching at the University of Wisconsin; and Geshe Ugyen Tseten of Rikon, Switzerland.[48]

In between meetings Merton recognized that he had come to appreciate the hermitage in Gethsemani, having realized that even in the Himalayas there were many people around and lots of noise.[49] He read some Bengali poetry as he rested between his first and second meetings with the Dalai Lama.[50]

Their second meeting took place on 6 November 1968 at 8.30 a.m., and they discussed epistemology and the mind, particularly Tibetan and Western Thomist theories.[51] Later, they discussed meditation, and the Dalai Lama showed Merton the essential position for meditation in Tibetan Buddhism whereby 'the right hand (discipline) is above the left (wisdom)', while in Zen Buddhism it is the other way around.[52] Merton commented on the Dalai Lama's way of thinking as follows:

> I like the solidity of the Dalai Lama's ideas. He is a very consecutive thinker and moves from step to step. His ideas of the interior life are built on very solid foundations and on a real awareness of practical problems.[53]

They also discussed the focusing of the mind on a particular object, and the possibilities and impossibilities of focusing on the mind as an object of meditation.[54] For Merton it was clear that the Dalai Lama missed the full monastic life and more time to study. It was the Dalai Lama who suggested a third meeting to discuss Western monasticism, and Merton agreed to come back and to think more about the issue of the mind, something the Dalai Lama wanted to discuss again.

In between meetings Merton continued reading Buddhist philosophy and reflecting on the renewal of monasticism. He wrote in his diary: 'The contemplative life must provide an area, a space of liberty, of silence, in which possibilities are allowed to surface and new choices – beyond routine choice – become manifest.'[55] Merton visited Chobgye Thicchen Rimpoche, a lama and poet of the Sakyapa school and, according to Merton, a great mystic.[56] They discussed meditation with an object and without an object. The lama asked Merton to outline for him the basis of Christian meditation and he wrote a poem for Merton and Merton did the same for him.[57]

The third meeting between Merton and the Fourteenth Dalai Lama took place on 8 November 1968, and they discussed Western monastic life, vows, dietary prohibitions and so on.[58] Merton raised monasticism and Marxism, the topic of his Bangkok lecture, and the Dalai Lama, who admired Marxism, suggested that 'from a certain point of view it was impossible for monks and Communists to get along, but that perhaps it should not be entirely impossible *if* Marxism meant *only* the establishment of an equitable economic and social structure'.[59]

It is clear that Merton's diaries provide only a short sketch of their conversations and that the actual sense of a personal conversation is missing for the readers and would have been expanded by Merton later in writings and conferences. However, it is possible to suggest that at the end of Merton's conversations with the Dalai Lama there was a natural closeness and a spiritual bond between them. Later, in his own autobiography the Dalai Lama recognized that the death of Merton had deprived the world of the possibility of a meaningful dialogue between Christians and Buddhists with all their ongoing similarities.[60] Nevertheless, it is clear that the meetings between Merton and the Dalai Lama had provided a sign of the Second Vatican Council's clear statement to the effect that all human beings 'form but one community'.[61]

Merton's destruction of the stranger

When in 1995 the Fourteenth Dalai Lama visited Merton's grave at Gethsemani, he meditated there accompanied by Abbot Timothy Kelly OCSO.[62] Thus, three decades later, the conversation between Merton and the Fourteenth Dalai Lama was resumed. In the words of the Fourteenth Dalai Lama: 'I am now in touch with his spirit.'[63] The fact is that the conversations about the spiritual path that had taken place between Merton and the Dalai Lama made them aware of *a common spiritual experience*. The commonality did not come from the possibility of discussing notions of a divine being, as Buddhists do not uphold creation out of an act by a divine being, but from a notion of emptiness. The spiritual commonality of a Buddhist monk and that of a Cistercian monk lies in the act of self-emptying. For the Buddhist, the emptying is conducive to an awareness of the power of the mind in fostering enlightenment, and in the particular case of Tibetan Buddhists such an empty-ing is conducive to an attitude of compassion and communion with all sentient beings, human and animal alike. For the Cister-cian monk, the act of self-emptying comes from the giving of oneself to God and to a community with the monastic stability of not leaving a group of monks for the rest of one's life.

Tsong-Kha-Pa (1357–1419), founder of the Gelug school of Tibetan Buddhism, the order of the Dalai Lama, stated clearly within the instructions for daily meditation that the following supplication should be recited many times: 'Please bless all living beings.'[64] The daily reality of meditation, which in Buddhism is not the sole realm of the celibate monk, creates the possibility of an opening to others and indeed to all, even enemies who through their hostile actions teach the Buddhist practitioner about the realities of suffering, the causes of and the remedies to all human suffering.[65] However, unlike in the Zen Buddhism dear to Merton, practitioners locate themselves in the realm of all sentient beings, so that Soname Yangchen, a Tibetan singer in exile, asserts quite clearly the aim of her daily meditation:

> I prayed for the end of suffering for all sentient beings. I visu-alised my family, my friends, my enemies and as many faceless strangers as I could sitting around me, and 'saw' the Buddha emanating streams of healing golden light, filling us with love, compassion and wisdom.[66]

The experience of the contemplative Catholic, a Cistercian monk, is not different as he seeks the love and manifestation of God through meditation. However, a common spiritual experience between a Buddhist monk and a Catholic monk did not mean that their contexts and paths were identical but that Merton and the Fourteenth Dalai Lama shared the common call of all human beings to acknowledge a spiritual path and a spiritual experience that makes all human beings share *a common path through different contexts*. This common call is expressed in the Buddhist compassion for all sentient beings and in the Christian love for all human beings. Both are realized through the hospitality shown by members of monastic communities to visitors, who are merely strangers in need of affirmation and human examples of an ongoing appreciation of a spiritual world that becomes real and tangible through the experience of practitioners. Those practitioners such as Merton did not solely show *kindness and compassion to strangers* but in doing so over a period of time minimized and finally destroyed the possibility of perceiving other human beings as 'strangers'.

The lessons of the encounter between Merton and the Fourteenth Dalai Lama remain central to contemporary life in that in a globalized society and a globalized spiritual experience there is an inherent danger: not to perceive strangers kindly. Merton's challenge is to destroy once and for all that category of 'otherness' and to replace it with an ongoing commonality that surpasses all differences and that is dictated by a daily search for the spiritual and for the contemplative experience of a common 'otherness' in every stranger. It is Merton's example of the study of other faiths and service to the stranger in our lives that remains a challenge for many contemporary Christians and Buddhists. This challenge becomes central to a globalized world to which the writings of Merton and his Asian journey have still a lot to offer. In Merton's words: 'attention must be concentrated on what is really essential to the monastic quest: this, I think, is to be sought in the area of true self-transcendence and enlightenment.'[67] These words and understanding remain central to contemporary reflections on relations between Christians and Buddhists as strangers today. However, let's return to Merton's journey in Asia.

Further meditations

After his third meeting with the Fourteenth Dalai Lama, Merton departed by jeep to Pathankot, where he took the train back to Delhi. There he spent the weekend. In Delhi he stayed at the Imperial Hotel, visited a Moslem college and said Mass at the Holy Family Hospital in the room where James George, the Canadian High Commissioner, was staying after a minor operation. At the same time he finished his talk for Bangkok and wrote to Dom Flavian, requesting permission to return to the USA via Europe. From Calcutta he sent a newsletter to Brother Patrick Hart so that he would mimeograph it and send it to friends and associates, mainly narrating his meetings with the Dalai Lama.[68] In one of his final thoughts about his encounters in Asia, Merton wrote: 'It is invaluable to have direct contact with people who have really put in a lifetime of hard work in training their minds and liberating themselves from passion and illusion.'[69] Then, off to Calcutta again, where he was much more impressed by the city and also saw the poverty and inequality around him.

On 12 November, Merton flew from Calcutta to Bagdogra over the mountains and then travelled by road to the Windamere Hotel in Darjeeling. Merton found the atmosphere too busy ('coenobitic') but enjoyed the cooler feel of the place.[70] On 13 November he said Mass at the Loreto Convent that was beside the hotel, and had coffee with the sisters.[71]

Since the Chinese invasion of Tibet, Darjeeling had remained a place where many Tibetan refugees lived, simply because it is located at a high altitude. It must be remembered that when the first Tibetan refugees started arriving in India the government provided generous help, land and the possibilities of opening schools where children could learn in Tibetan.

However, land that was readily available was in low-altitude fields, mostly south of the Himalayas. Many Tibetan refugees who were sent there got ill and died. Thus, the Indian Government decided to welcome refugees into higher and cooler areas such as Darjeeling, which became a large centre for Tibetan refugees and later for their children. Merton visited the Tibetan Refugee Centre on 14 November and described it as 'a happy and busy place'.[72] On the same day he visited St Joseph's School in North Point. By 15 November Merton was enjoying his time in Darjeeling and stayed at a tea plantation, the Mim Tea Estate, as well as the Tibetan monastery led by the abbot, Drugpa Thugsey Rimpoche.[73] The abbot was out but they had tea in his cell and Merton remarked that he had 'a sense that something very real went on in here, in spite of the poverty and squalor'.[74]

There is no doubt that the Merton who had left the USA for his journey to Asia had been transformed by meeting the Fourteenth Dalai Lama, and certainly the talks he was planning to give in Thailand were only a necessary completion of a journey that would have been unthinkable for him many years before. For the journey of a lifetime was going to be only a mirror of another lifetime journey; once again Merton was able to combine his personal contemplation with a daily familiarization with the events around him and with the daily realities of overactive people living in an overpopulated continent. It was only his death that would stop his earthly journey and would make his exit from a meeting with other contemplatives much more surprising and intriguing – a death in Thailand that even Merton the all-knowing could not have predicted.

Conclusion:
Merton's lessons for today

Contemplation in daily life

There is one danger in reading Merton's life: the possibility of making a sharp distinction between the contemplative calling and the active calling within Christian life, to understand a life of intense prayer as completely different from an active life of Christian service in society. Thus, it is possible for a reader of Merton's work to decide that Merton's life, while important for those living a secluded religious life, has nothing to do with the life of discipleship of other Christians who are married or have a relationship and live in the world with a job and the daily care of children and family dependants. If the present reader were to think thus, the exploration of Merton's life in the chapters of this book would not have achieved its purpose. For the purpose of examining the life of a prominent contemplative, writer and monk is to affirm others who are trying to do the same and to show the richness of a Christian who made a difference for others; he pursued the ultimate human activity: the search for the Creator and for others as images of the living God.

Merton's life culminates with his final encounter with the Father on the day he died in Thailand, after delivering a special lecture on 'Marxism and Monastic Activities'.[1] It is very appropriate to end the examination of his life and draw some conclusions by looking at some of Merton's thoughts in this lecture, because Merton chose to deliver it and because he was at the pinnacle of his own journey in search of God. That journey had started with his reception into the Catholic

Church in New York, had taken shape over years at the Abbey of Gethsemani and ended in Thailand with his death on 10 December 1968.[2]

Contemplation and human activity

During 1968, Merton had been attending a conference at the Center for the Study of Democratic Institutions in Santa Barbara, California, where the participants were revolutionary university leaders from France, Italy, Germany and the Low Countries.[3] In informal conversation with them, Merton had discussed monasticism and Marxism, and one of the French students told him: 'We are also monks.'[4] It is unclear to me why Merton thought that this student and others were saying to him: 'We are the true monks. You are not the true monks; we are the true monks', but this is the statement that Merton takes for his reflection on monks, Marxists and monasticism.[5] Indeed, Merton opened the lecture by arguing that a young monk in a process of 'identity crisis' needs to ask about his identity in all contemporary contexts, including that of a dialogue and a challenge by a Marxist.[6]

Merton concerned himself not with orthodox Marxism, presumably the early writings by Karl Marx, nor with the political application of Marxism, presumably the application of Marxist thought in the 1917 Soviet revolution, but with what he called 'a kind of mystique of Marxism'.[7] He relied heavily on a neo-Marxist interpretation of Marx by Herbert Marcuse, the 'father of the new left' in the USA, whom he regarded as 'a kind of monastic thinker', and on 'the monastic implications of Marcuse at the present moment'.[8]

Merton's use of Marcuse in the text of his lecture is quite sudden, however, Merton deals with an author and a Marxist who was influential in the lives and minds of the youth and intellectuals within a common theme or social or theoretical problem: that of alienation in society.[9] Marcuse as a university professor had made a tremendous impact by supporting and taking part in 1960s student protests. Young intellectuals in the universities and Marxists alike, influenced by Marcuse, argued that the choices, 'significant choices', could no longer be made in organized societies led by capitalism or under Soviet influences but were (and are) made by individuals who escape a state of personal alienation.[10]

Merton's emphasis on the possibilities of changing individual human beings rather than institutions allowed him to deliver a lecture on a topic that could have seemed to be completely out of place within a group of contemplative leaders. However, Merton's genius shows precisely in the unexpected. It is the discipline of neo-Marxists to challenge structures that he is identifying with, despite the fact that institutions are identified with both the Soviet revolution and the reform of monasticism, the latter within medieval time as well as at the time of the Second Vatican Council.

In delivering a lecture to the intellectual minds of Asia, backed by Marcuse as 'a monastic thinker', Merton made a formal address, a referential testament of his personal concerns that was very different in form from his writings and his style of addressing participants at his conferences. He told his audience:

> I am addressing myself to the monk who is potentially open to contact with the intellectual, the university student, the university professor, the people who are thinking along lines that are going to change both Western and Eastern society and create the world of the future, in which inevitably we are going to have to make our adaptation.[11]

If those were Merton's initial words, almost his last words of the conference were 'so I will disappear', giving a dramatic exit from Merton's conference and an end to a life of spoken words. It was a fitting end to a lecture that was a kind of testament of contemplation and material–human activity, of Christianity and Marxism, of renewal and continuity, a truly dialectic confer-ence.[12] I cannot help relating Merton's lecture to the farewell of another Marxist similar to Marcuse, Salvador Allende, who exited a few years later on the day of the Chilean military coup. On 11 September 1973, Allende remained at the Chilean Presidential Palace of La Moneda as the plotting troops sur-rounded it. As the bombardment continued he addressed particular people, as Merton did, with a style for a historical occasion that needs to be marked by formal words, delivered for history.[13] In part of his final address through Magallanes Radio, Allende spoke thus:

> I am addressing myself to the humble woman of this land, to the female worker who worked harder, to the mother who understood our concern for children. I am addressing myself to professionals of this land, patriot professionals, those who until recently were challenging the fascist attitudes of the profes-sional colleges ... I am addressing myself to the youth, those who sang, those who offered their happiness and their fighting spirit ... I am addressing myself to the Chilean man, to the worker, to the peasant, to the intellectual and those who will be persecuted.[14]

The form of public address used by Allende was so close to that of Merton that one could only suggest that it follows the pattern of those who are about to die giving up their life for their ideals. Indeed, Merton's last conference was a farewell to fellow contemplatives rather than a teaching moment by a wise teacher. As both Marcuse and Allende did, Merton located himself in the place of the young looking for identity, and felt that the professionals and intellectuals – despised by spiritual people, traditional Marxists and capitalists – were the ones who could hear the words, who could 'listen' as in the beginning of the *Rule of St Benedict* and continue carrying the torch by changing themselves first and then the structures that sheltered them.

It is this possibility of removing 'alienation' from religious practice and academic life that united Merton and Marcuse, and Merton's lecture outlined the particular contribution of the Jesuit, Teilhard de Chardin, banned from publishing by the Vatican because of his thought on the material world, but studied and accepted by Marxist scholars.[15] For Marxism, according to Merton, all knowledge and action is centred on matter, and an understanding of economic processes is much needed in order to understand the development of human beings.[16] This was a bold statement by Merton as Teilhard de Chardin had been silenced because of the challenges that his non-linear reading of the book of Genesis had for the Catholic doctrine of original sin.

However, Merton recognized in his lecture that there were three disciplines that were outside Marxist concepts of society's understanding because of their avoidance of the centrality of matter: religion, philosophy and politics.[17] Merton's dialogue with Marxism indicated that they were unified by a critique of the established and traditional Marxism and Christianity that had made religion and politics oppressive for the aspirations of those who didn't participate in a capitalistic world of profit, earnings and power/control over souls, in a process of 'alienation' that once again unified neo-Marxists and progressive contemplatives within the Church.

According to Merton, what was important for a real movement towards Christian–Marxist dialogue was the contribution of Buddhist and Christian monks, the contemplatives within religious traditions in which the building of monastic communities starts with the making of a person from the inside, indeed it starts 'with man's own consciousness'.[18] 'Ignorance' in Buddhism and 'alienation' in Marxism find their negative equivalent here in the ignorance of 'myth', where everything is explained through 'myth', for example, the case of 'original sin'.[19] Merton is clear at this point that he is not trying to discredit the doctrine of original sin, but that this concept has been used to explain all sorts of unexplained points of ignorance. (Merton is afraid here that he could be labelled a heretic with Teilhard de Chardin.) Thus, the concept of ignorance in Christianity is very similar to ignorance in Buddhism, as both of them suggest an inability to seek enlightenment and a more solid explanation that arises out of the self. Merton argues very concretely that the Christian and the Buddhist monk share the same traditional purpose of the traditional religions; religions that 'begin with the consciousness of the individual, seek to transform and liberate the truth in each person, with the idea that it will then communicate itself to others'.[20]

The monk, Christian or Buddhist:

> dwells in the centre of society as one who has attained realization . . . he has come to experience the ground of his own being in such a way that he knows the secret of liberation and can somehow or other communicate this to others.[21]

Ultimately, monastic life connects with Marxism because the way of monastic learning is a change, in traditional Augustinian terms, from *cupiditas* into *caritas*, from self-centred love into an outgoing, unselfish love.[22] In the case of Marxism and in Merton's analysis, there is a change from capitalist greed to communal communism, in a material order in which each one gives according to capacities and receives according to needs.[23] However, for Merton the only place where this communist sharing can be done and realized is in a monastery.[24]

Merton finally reaches some conclusions in his lecture and he argues very strongly that monasticism and the act of learning how to love remains central to human life despite monastic institutions, because monastic institutions can fade away but the human inner longing for transformation and for a school of love remains.[25] And for Merton that school of monasticism respects plurality, it learns from other traditions and asserts the possibility of a religious commitment based on compassion and not on ignorance. Religious diversity and the school of love becomes for Merton the path of monasticism and of Christian life. Marxism, and the work of Marcuse, even when poorly developed in Merton's lecture, bring the materiality of love for others and for other religious traditions, because it is in contact with others and with respect for world religions that the call to contemplation takes place.

That call to love and to exercise a school of love becomes a Christian call that does not remain isolated in Christianity but is a call for all other world religions. Thus, in an essay written before his Asian journey and reprinted as an appendix to the *Asian Journal of Thomas Merton*, Merton wrote about the *Bhagavadgītā*, the sacred Hindu text, and concluded: 'The *Gita*, like the Gospels, teaches us to live in awareness of an inner truth that exceeds the grasp of our thought and cannot be subject to our own control.'[26] It is love that brings war to a dialectic materialist dialogue in the *Gita*; it is love that brings the Christian to learn and to cooperate with Marxists and practitioners of other world religions. Merton's prayer at the First Spiritual Summit Conference in Calcutta says it all. Merton prayed from a text saying, 'I ask you to concentrate on the love that is in you, that is in us all', and later in his extempore prayer Merton asserted: 'You witness to the ultimate reality that is love. Love has overcome. Love is victorious.'[27]

Contemplation and political activity

Merton's stress on Marxist theory in his Thailand lecture related not to a fashion but to his own engagement with philosophical thought that was central for the 1968 understanding of the world. French Marxism of the neo-Marxist strand of Louis Althusser had dominated a new kind of material understanding of political action in French and US society at that time.[28] The French Communist Party, still very strong, was keen to reactivate the power of the unions, and a change of outlook in French institutions aided intellectuals and theoreticians. The 1968 discussions and consequent protests about the role of French universities pushed a certain immediacy of French Marxist theory. For it was clear that French Marxism was independent of the Soviet Union and the Russian revolution's centralized political power, and at the same time opposed to the US model of society based on antagonisms of the cold war and a trickle down of economic benefits to the infrastructure of society through a private sense of financial capital.

Political activity within French Marxism was people-centred and even challenged the power of the state by incorporating intellectuals and thinkers who became parts of the infrastructure (in Marxist vocabulary) and not of the superstructure. For it was knowledge given to all that changed the state and not the elimination of intellectuals who had been perceived as members of an oppressive structure. Once education was given to all, intellectuals, thinkers and writers changed theoretically from the oppressive superstructure into the liberating infrastructure. Thus, the change was theoretical within neo-Marxism and not pragmatic; it was in the realm of the imagination of social institutions rather than in the return to the original Marxist understandings of the nineteenth century or the hard applications based on the totalitarian experience of the Soviet Union and the People's Republic of China (an aspect of French Marxism criticized by Althusser).

Merton's use of Marxism in a lecture to other contemplatives set a pace that was rather different from solely a path of renewal stressed and normatively implemented by the Second Vatican Council. He referred to Marxism as a philosophical and materialistic view of the world centred in 'matter'. However, he did not outline a change of social structures as the only solution to society, to religion or to politics. Instead, he proposed a change in one's heart and experience, that is the 'disalienation' of the 'new man', a 'new man' fostered by socialist projects such as that of Salvador Allende in 1970s Chile and mentioned by the apostle Paul in relation to baptism and a new life in Christ. Thus, Merton's 'impressionistic treatment' of Marxism realized what others had not managed: the correlation of the change of self with structures in Marxism, Christianity, Buddhism and Hinduism.[29]

Merton's lessons for today

The first lesson of Merton's life and trip to Asia was his constant contemplation. Although he didn't write more about his personal prayer in the diaries, his death also prevented us from reading any other works by him. Nevertheless, it is very clear that he enjoyed and savoured moments of tranquillity and contemplation while in Asia and that, regardless of his punishing journey from one place to another, he enjoyed the quiet of his conversation with God. At the Mim Tea State, for example, he wrote: 'I finished Murti on Madhyamika, meditated, sometimes sleepily, and was entirely content.'[30]

After his stay at Darjeeling, Merton journeyed back to Calcutta and from there he flew to Madras, where he stayed from 26 to 28 November 1968.[31] After visiting beaches and Hindu temples in Madras, Merton continued to Ceylon, where he stayed from 29 November to 6 December 1968.[32] Then off to Singapore, where he was happy about the restaurants he was taken to but was not happy about the noise, and described Singapore as 'the city of transistors, tape recorders, cameras, perfumes, silk shirts, fine liquors . . .'[33] By then he was not looking forward to the meeting in Bangkok and he noted that 'certainly I am sick of hotels and planes'.[34]

On 7 December 1968 Merton arrived in Bangkok and went to see the Temple of the Emerald Buddha.[35] Most of the delegates arrived in Bangkok on 8 December and Merton met some of them and went to look for Dom Leclercq, to move to the Red Cross site 30 kilometres out of Bangkok where the meeting was to take place and where they were staying.[36]

If the first contribution by Merton was his capacity to be a contemplative while enjoying or facing whatever happened around him, his second contribution is clearly manifested in one of his diaries' comments on arrival at the meeting. A Dutch abbot wanted Merton to give a television interview because this would be good for the Church. Merton declined and his comment was sharp, measured and critical: 'It would be much "better for the church" if I refrained.'[37] Merton was a good Cistercian and made an enormous contribution to the media and society's respect for the Catholic Church, but he rejected the idea of becoming a product, something that had already worried him at Gethsemani, the abbey that profited from all his royalties and rights. Merton the contemplative was ready to be critical of his own fame, even when he was a man who liked to be praised for what he did and wrote.

Merton, the media-prodigy-to-be, while in Bangkok walked past the post office and visited a Buddhist temple in Chinatown.[38] To finish the day and to show his enjoyment of life, Merton had a Hungarian dinner and went to the cinema. It is possible to think that Merton 'the tourist' was having a break from his obligations as a monk; however, he did not see it this way. His diary reflects the daily activities that were different for him while all along there are hints that he celebrated Mass, said his office and longed for more hours to contemplate, to be on his own, and especially to read.[39] However, the contemplative Merton enjoyed his busy life and on 8 December, the Feast of the Immaculate Conception, he said Mass at St Louis Church and had lunch at the Apostolic Delegation before moving to the Red Cross Centre in the afternoon.

A third important contribution to the Church's awareness of its time was centralized and channelled in Merton's love of diversity. He was not a scholar, in the sense of an academic searching for answers to academic questions, but a monk, trying to discover life and spiritual life outside the confines of an abbey in Kentucky. His literary and academic talent was channelled into a few hours of study and later into a deeper awareness of God. Love for diversity did not make him afraid of searching for truth outside the confines of his own tradition but, once he realized that there was diversity everywhere, he understood quickly that those traditions were pointing to the same deep spiritual search for the enlightened self that was able to dwell on the manifestations of the divine and the presence of God in the world, in other manifestations of spirituality and in diverse human beings.

The influence of Merton remains strong among some sectors of the Christian Church, and Merton's contribution is of importance for Christian communities today. Themes to be explored at any time within Merton's writings remain: the welcoming of strangers, contemplation and political activism, lives of contemplation, the silence of God and the contemporary issues of nuclear weapons, ecology, global warming and globalization. If Merton did not perceive himself as a spiritual teacher, there is no doubt that he centred anybody around him in two powerful divine and human realities: love and diversity. These themes, attitudes and Christian values remain strong points of Christian life today in an era of globalization, an era that Merton tried to grasp in his Asian journey and that, in my opinion, he would have liked.

Notes

———— ·•·•·• ————

Introduction: Merton the contemplative activist

1 Abbot Robert Barnes OCSO, 'Remembering Father Flavian at Berryville: Homily at the Funeral Mass for Fr. Flavian Burns OCSO, October 17, 2005', *The Merton Seasonal* 31 (2006/1, Spring), pp. 23–5, at p. 24.

2 'Introduction' in John Richardson with the collaboration of Marilyn McCully, *A Life of Picasso, Vol. I: 1881–1906* (London: Jonathan Cape), 1996, p. 3.

3 For a history of the Abbey of Gethsemani see Dianne Aprile, *The Abbey of Gethsemani: Place of Peace and Paradox* (Louisville, KY: Trout Lilly Press), 1998; for the history of the Cistercians see Esther de Waal, *The Way of Simplicity: The Cistercian Tradition* (Maryknoll, NY: Orbis), 1998; James France, *The Cistercians in Medieval Art* (Kalamazoo, MI: Cistercian Publications), 1998; Louis Lekai, *The Cistercians: Ideals and Reality* (Kent, OH: Kent State University Press), 1977; André Louf, *The Cistercian Way* (Kalamazoo, MI: Cistercian Publications), 1983; and Patricia Matarasso (ed.), *The Cistercian World: Monastic Writings of the Twelfth Century* (London: Penguin), 1993.

4 Jim Forest, *Living with Wisdom: A Life of Thomas Merton* (Maryknoll, NY: Orbis), 1991, pp. 79–80.

5 Regarding the issue of diverse biographies it must be remembered that in 1967 Merton set up the Thomas Merton Legacy Trust, a legal agreement that didn't allow general access to Merton's diaries for 25 years with the exception of the trustees: Naomi Burton Stone (his literary agent), James Laughlin (his publisher at New Directions) and Tommie O'Callaghan (Mrs Frank O'Callaghan), and a few years later Robert Giroux replaced Stone within the board of trustees. An official biographer, John Howard Griffin, was appointed in 1969, however he became ill and in 1978 Michael Mott was appointed official biographer and wrote the authorized biography of Merton, *The Seven Mountains of Thomas Merton* (Boston, MA: Houghton Mifflin), 1984, later published in the UK (London: Sheldon Press, SPCK) in 1986.

Prior to this was Monica Furlong's biography, *Merton: A Biography* (London: Collins), 1980. Once all Merton's papers and diaries were available, a series of biographies followed, including Lawrence S. Cunningham, *Thomas Merton and the Monastic Vision* (Grand Rapids, MI and Cambridge: William B. Eerdmans), 1999; and a series of seven volumes with transcripts of Merton's diaries were published after the end of Merton's moratorium that legally ended on 10 December 1993; see 'Preface' in Patrick Hart OCSO (ed.), *Run to the Mountain: The Story of a Vocation – The Journals of Thomas Merton*, vol. 1, 1939–41 (New York: HarperCollins), 1996, p. xi.

6 Merton's memories of his mother were of a strict woman and, according to Monica Furlong, 'there is always a faint bitterness in his references to her; she seemed critical, pedagogic, "severe", measuring him all the time against some standard that seemed unattainable, leaving him with a sour taste of failure, and of being inadequate', *Merton: A Biography*, pp. 13–15, at p. 15.

7 Mott, *Seven Mountains of Thomas Merton*, pp. 50–2.

8 Thomas Merton, *The Seven Storey Mountain* (London: SPCK, 1990), pp. 71–2.

9 Merton, *Seven Storey Mountain*.

10 Merton had attended some of those Communist meetings and at one of them had signed as a member of the Young Communist League, taking the party name Frank Swift; Furlong, *Merton: A Biography*, p. 67.

11 Furlong, *Merton: A Biography*, p. 67.

12 Even after years in Gethsemani Merton followed Maritain's writings and life; see Merton's diary entry 23 October 1963, where he writes: 'The rumour goes around that Maritain has been made a Cardinal. John Howard Griffin even declares he has seen this in print', in Robert E. Daggy (ed.), *Dancing in the Water of Life: Seeking Peace in the Hermitage – The Journals of Thomas Merton*, vol. 5, 1963–5 (New York: HarperCollins), 1997, p. 26.

13 Merton, *Seven Storey Mountain*, p. 316.

14 Merton had been previously rejected as a conscript because of his teeth, but because of the impending conflict with Japan the US Army was drafting thousands of young Americans and the local secretary of the draft board told him that under the new pressures he most probably would be drafted into the army; see Mott, *Seven Mountains of Thomas Merton*, p. 200.

15 Merton, *Seven Storey Mountain*, p. 378.

16 Cunningham, *Thomas Merton and the Monastic Vision*, p. 22.

17 9 April 1941 Wednesday in Holy Week at Our Lady of Gethsemani, in Hart (ed.) *Run to the Mountain*, p. 340.

18 Merton published a history of his religious order under the title *The Waters of Siloe* (New York: Harcourt, Brace & Company), 1949.

19 Thomas Merton, *The Sign of Jonas* (San Diego, New York and London: Harcourt, Brace & Company), 1979.

20 Merton, *Sign of Jonas*, p. 361.

21 Thomas Merton, *Conjectures of a Guilty Bystander* (New York and London: Image Books Doubleday), 1989.

22 'Introduction' in Lawrence S. Cunningham (ed.), *A Search for Solitude: Pursuing the Monk's True Life – The Journals of Thomas Merton*, vol. 3, 1952–60 (New York: HarperCollins), 1996, p. xvi.

23 *The Rule of Saint Benedict*, trans. Leonard Doyle (Collegeville, MN: Liturgical Press), 2001, p. 53, cf. Matthew 25.35.

24 Merton, *Seven Storey Mountain*, p. 321.

25 See Austin Flannery OP (ed.), *Vatican Council II: The Conciliar and Post Conciliar Documents* (Northport, NY: Costello; Grand Rapids, MI: William B. Eerdmans), 1992.

26 See Pope John XXIII's speech calling a council on 25 March 1959, when he spoke of 'the Church of the poor', and in his own will under the section 'My last will concerning things which belong to me as patriarch of Venice' he wrote 'My crosses and rings likewise are to be sold so as to fetch the highest possible price and the proceeds from these also given to the poor in whatever seems the most suitable form', Castel Gandolfo, 12 September 1961, in Pope John XXIII, *Journal of a Soul* (London: Geoffrey Chapman), 1980, p. 370.

27 Thomas Merton, *Conjectures of a Guilty Bystander*, part II, 'Truth and Violence: An Interesting Era', pp. 63–128.

28 Merton, *Conjectures of a Guilty Bystander*, p. 78.

29 See ongoing correspondence between Cardenal and Merton in *Del Monasterio al Mundo: Correspondencia entre Ernesto Cardenal y Thomas Merton* (Santiago, Chile: Editorial Cuarto Propio), 1998; and materials related to the experimental lay contemplative community founded by Cardenal on the Nicaraguan island of Solentiname in Ernesto Cardenal, *El Evangelio en Solentiname* (Salamanca: Ediciones Sígueme), 1976 and *El Evangelio en Solentiname: Volumen Segundo* (Salamanca: Ediciones Sígueme), 1978; see also Mario I. Aguilar, *The History and Politics of Latin American Theology* I (London: SCM Press), 2007, ch. 5, pp. 91–104.

30 30 October 1964 in Daggy (ed.), *Dancing in the Water of Life*, p. 159.

31 *Gaudium et Spes* 1.

32 Mario I. Aguilar, *Contemplating God, Changing the World* (London: SPCK), 2008.

33 Jonathan Montaldo, 'Foreword' to John Eudes Bamberger OCSO, *Thomas Merton: Prophet of Renewal* (Kalamazoo, MI: Cistercian Publications), 2005, pp. vii–xii, at pp. x–xi.

34 See for example, James Baker, *Thomas Merton: Social Critic* (Lexington, KY: University of Kentucky Press), 1971; Ross Labrie, *The Art of Thomas Merton* (Forth Worth, TX: Texas Christian University Press), 1979; Elena Malits, *The Solitary Explorer: Thomas Merton's Transforming Journey* (San Francisco: Harper), 1980; Gerald Twomey, *Thomas Merton: Prophet in the Belly of a Paradox* (New York: Paulist), 1978; Victor Kramer, *Thomas Merton: Monk and Artist* (Kalamazoo, MI: Cistercian Publications), 1987; Jim Forest, *Thomas Merton: A Pictorial Biography* (New York: Paulist), 1980, reissued as *Living with Wisdom* (Maryknoll, NY: Orbis), 1991; Ralph Eugene Meatyard (ed.), *Father Louie: Portraits of Thomas Merton* (New York: Tinken), 1971; Anthony Padovano, *The Human Journey: Thomas Merton, Symbol of a Century* (Garden City, NY: Doubleday), 1982; Patrick Hart OSCO (ed.), *Thomas Merton: Monk* (New York: Sheed & Ward), 1974; Therese Lentfoehr, *Words and Silence: On the Poetry of Thomas Merton* (New York: New Directions), 1979; George Kilcourse, *Ace of Freedoms: Thomas Merton's Christ* (Notre Dame: University of Notre Dame Press), 1993; George Woodcock, *Thomas Merton: Monk and Poet – A Critical Study* (New York: Farrar, Straus & Giroux), 1978; David D. Cooper, *Thomas Merton's Art of Denial: The Evolution of a Radical Humanist* (Athens, GA: University of Georgia Press), 1989; and Paul Pearson et al. (eds)., *Thomas Merton: Poet-Monk-Prophet* (Abergavenny, UK: Three Peaks Press), 1998.

35 Bamberger OCSO, *Thomas Merton: Prophet of Renewal*, p. 79.

36 On the conversation of Merton and the Fourteenth Dalai Lama see Mario Aguilar Benítez, *The Stranger in Thomas Merton and the 14th Dalai Lama* (Santiago: Fundación Literaria Civilización), 2010.

1 A contemplative teacher

1 The major holding of Merton's papers is the Thomas Merton Center at Bellarmine University in Louisville, Kentucky, and there are other

papers at the libraries of Saint Bonaventure's University in Olean, New York, and at Columbia University in New York.

2 Lawrence S. Cunningham (ed.), *A Search for Solitude: Pursuing the Monk's True Life – The Journals of Thomas Merton*, vol. 3, 1952–60 (New York: HarperCollins), 1996, p. 15.

3 See for example the following books by Merton: *The Last of the Fathers* (New York: Harcourt Brace & Company), 1954; *No Man Is an Island* (New York: Harcourt Brace & Company), 1955; *The Living Bread* (New York: Farrar, Straus & Cudahy), 1956; *The Silent Life* (New York: Harcourt Brace & Company), 1957; *Thoughts in Solitude* (New York: Harcourt Brace & Company), 1958; *The Secular Journal of Thomas Merton* (New York: Farrar, Straus & Company), 1959; and *Disputed Questions* (New York: Farrar, Straus & Company), 1960.

4 10 March 1953 in Cunningham (ed.), *A Search for Solitude*, p. 41.

5 Letter from Thomas Merton to Mark van Doren, 7 April 1953; Robert E. Daggy (ed.), *The Road to Joy: The Letters of Thomas Merton to New and Old Friends* (New York: Farrar, Straus & Giroux), 1989, pp. 24–5, at p. 24.

6 10 October 1952 in Cunningham (ed.), *A Search for Solitude*, p. 19.

7 Thomas Merton, *The Waters of Siloe* (New York: Harcourt, Brace & Company), 1949.

8 22 October 1952 in Cunningham (ed.), *A Search for Solitude*, p. 15.

9 See 'Some Bibliographical Notes' in Lawrence S. Cunningham, *Thomas Merton and the Monastic Vision* (Grand Rapids, MI and Cambridge: William B. Eerdmans), 1999, pp. 211–25.

10 13 September 1952 in Cunningham (ed.), *A Search for Solitude*, p. 15.

11 26 September 1952 in Cunningham (ed.), *A Search for Solitude*, p. 18.

12 Daggy (ed.), *Road to Joy*, p. 25.

13 Letter from Merton to Sister Therese Lentfoehr SDS, 20 May 1953 in Daggy (ed.), *Road to Joy*, p. 213.

14 29 November 1952 in Cunningham (ed.), *Search for Solitude*, p. 25.

15 14 January 1953 in Cunningham (ed.), *Search for Solitude*, p. 28.

16 12 February 1953 in Cunningham (ed.), *Search for Solitude*, p. 30.

17 10 October 1952 in Cunningham (ed.), *Search for Solitude*, p. 20.

18 30 August 1957 in William H. Shannon (ed.), *Witness to Freedom: The Letters of Thomas Merton in Times of Crisis* (New York: Harvest), 1995, pp. 161–2, at p. 162.

19 20 August 1956 in Cunningham (ed.), *Search for Solitude*, p. 69.

20 29 August 1957 in Cunningham (ed.), *Search for Solitude*, p. 114.

21 27 December 1957 in Cunningham (ed.), *Search for Solitude*, p. 149.

22 12 January 1958 in Cunningham (ed.), *Search for Solitude*, p. 154.

23 14 January 1958 in Cunningham (ed.), *Search for Solitude*, p. 155.

24 30 July 1957 in Cunningham (ed.), *Search for Solitude*, p. 103.

25 17 September 1957 in Cunningham (ed.), *Search for Solitude*, p. 120.

26 29 August 1957 in Cunningham (ed.), *Search for Solitude*, p. 113.

27 24 December 1957 in Cunningham (ed.), *Search for Solitude*, p. 148.

28 10 December 1957 in Cunningham (ed.), *Search for Solitude*, p. 145.

29 23 January 1958 in Cunningham (ed.), *Search for Solitude*, p. 159.

30 28 February 1958 in Cunningham (ed.), *Search for Solitude*, p. 175.

31 23 March 1958 in Cunningham (ed.), *Search for Solitude*, p. 183.

32 3 August 1957 in Cunningham (ed.), *Search for Solitude*, p. 105.

33 8 August 1957 in Cunningham (ed.), *Search for Solitude*, p. 107.

34 26 November 1957 in Cunningham (ed.), *Search for Solitude*, p. 143.

35 26 November 1957 in Cunningham (ed.), *Search for Solitude*, p. 144.

36 6 January 1958 in Cunningham (ed.), *Search for Solitude*, p. 153.

37 14 January 1958 in Cunningham (ed.), *Search for Solitude*, p. 155.

38 31 January 1958 in Cunningham (ed.), *Search for Solitude*, p. 163.

39 9 February 1958 in Cunningham (ed.), *Search for Solitude*, p. 165.

40 31 December 1957 in Cunningham (ed.), *Search for Solitude*, pp. 152–3.

41 Jaramillo turned up at the abbey unexpectedly on 21 February 1958 (see Merton's narrative in Cunningham (ed.), *Search for Solitude*, pp. 173–4) and immediately caught the epidemic flu of the abbey; entry of 27 February 1958, p. 174.

42 24 January 1958 in Cunningham (ed.), *Search for Solitude*, pp. 159–60.

43 15 February 1958 in Cunningham (ed.), *Search for Solitude*, pp. 166–7.

44 11 February 1958 in Cunningham (ed.), *Search for Solitude*, p. 166.

45 22 October 1957 in Cunningham (ed.), *Search for Solitude*, pp. 126–7.

46 24 December 1957 in Cunningham (ed.), *Search for Solitude*, p. 147.

47 29 December 1957 in Cunningham (ed.), *Search for Solitude*, p. 150.

48 29 December 1957 in Cunningham (ed.), *Search for Solitude*, p. 150.

49 29 December 1957 in Cunningham (ed.), *Search for Solitude*, p. 150.

50 16 February 1958 in Cunningham (ed.), *Search for Solitude*, pp. 169–70.

51 15 February 1958 in Cunningham (ed.), *Search for Solitude*, p. 168.

52 Pablo Antonio Cuadra (1912–2002) was born on 4 November 1912 in Managua but spent most of his life in Granada. In 1931 he founded the Vanguardia poetic movement, together with the Nicaraguan poets José Coronel Urtecho and Joaquín Pasos. Cuadra published his *Poemas nicaragüenses* in 1934 and opposed the US intervention against Sandino in the 1930s. Later he was in the opposition to dictator Somoza and after 1979 he also criticized the policies on culture of the Sandinista Government. Later, he lived in exile in Costa Rica and Texas. He died in Managua having won the Gabriela Mistral Inter-American Cultural Prize awarded by the Organization of American States in 1991. His works include *Canto Temporal* (1943), *Poemas con un crepúsculo a cuestas* (1949), *La tierra prometida* (1952), *El jaguar y la luna* (1959), *Poesía* (1964), *Cantos de Cifar* (1971), *Esos rostros que asoman en la multitud* (1976), and *Siete árboles contra el atardecer* (1980).

53 3 May 1958 in Cunningham (ed.), *Search for Solitude*, p. 200.

54 17 December 1959 in Cunningham (ed.), *Search for Solitude*, p. 358.

55 17 December 1959 in Cunningham (ed.), *Search for Solitude*, p. 359.

2 A contemplative writer

1 Letter from Merton to Robert Menchin, 15 January 1966 in William H. Shannon (ed.), *Witness to Freedom: The Letters of Thomas Merton in Times of Crisis* (San Diego, New York and London: Harcourt Brace & Company), 1995, p. 254.

2 Letter from Merton to William Robert Miller, June 1962 in Shannon (ed.), *Witness to Freedom*, p. 249.

3 14 February 1960 in Lawrence S. Cunningham (ed.), *A Search for Solitude: Pursuing the Monk's True Life – The Journals of Thomas Merton*, vol. 3, 1952–60 (New York: HarperCollins), 1996, pp. 375–6.

4 19 February 1960 in Cunningham (ed.), *Search for Solitude*, p. 376.

5 8 May 1960 in Cunningham (ed.), *Search for Solitude*, p. 387.

6 31 January 1960 in Cunningham (ed.), *Search for Solitude*, p. 373.

7 'Introduction: Towards Crisis and Mystery' in Victor A. Kramer (ed.), *Turning toward the World: The Journals of Thomas Merton*, vol. 4, 1960–63 (New York: HarperCollins), 1996, p. xv.

8 Kramer (ed.), *Turning toward the World*, p. 3.

9 Kramer (ed.), *Turning toward the World*, p. 4.

10 5 June 1960 in Kramer (ed.), *Turning toward the World*, p. 6.

11 5 June 1960 in Kramer (ed.), *Turning toward the World*, p 7.

12 9 June 1960 in Kramer (ed.), *Turning toward the World*, p. 9. I mention this entry because as I write another large earthquake and tsunami happened in southern Chile on 27 February 2010.

13 For a biography of Mark van Doren see William H. Shannon, Christine M. Bochen and Patrick F. O'Connell (eds), *The Thomas Merton Encyclopedia* (Maryknoll, NY: Orbis), 2002, p. 503.

14 Some of their correspondence can be found in George Hendrick (ed.), *The Selected Letters of Mark Van Doren* (Baton Rouge: Louisiana State University Press), 1987; and in Robert E. Daggy (ed.), *The Road to Joy: The Letters of Thomas Merton to New and Old Friends* (New York: Farrar, Straus & Giroux), 1989, pp. 3–55.

15 Upon Merton's death Abbot Flavian Burns sent a telegram dated 11 December 1968 to all Merton's friends, including Van Doren, advising them of it; see Daggy (ed.), *Road to Joy*, 1989, p. 55.

16 Merton received the first copy of *Disputed Questions* on 3 September 1960; see Kramer (ed.), *Turning toward the World*, p. 40.

17 Letter from Merton to Mark van Doren, 17 September 1960, in Daggy (ed.), *Road to Joy*, p. 39.

18 Letter from Merton to Mark van Doren, 16 February 1961, in Daggy (ed.), *Road to Joy*, p. 40.

19 14 August 1960 in Kramer (ed.), *Turning toward the World*, p. 31.

20 Letter from Merton to Professor Jean Hering, 6 April 1964, in Daggy (ed.), *Road to Joy*, p. 61.

21 26 August 1960 in Kramer (ed.), *Turning toward the World*, p. 36.

22 Letter from Merton to Mark van Doren, 13 May 1961, in Daggy (ed.), *Road to Joy*, p. 41.

23 Daggy (ed.), *Road to Joy*, p. 41.

24 Letter from Merton to Mark van Doren, 13 May 1961, in Daggy (ed.), *Road to Joy*, p. 42.

25 Letter from Merton to Mark van Doren, 16 February 1961, in Daggy (ed.), *Road to Joy*, p. 40.

26 Daggy (ed.), *Road to Joy*, p. 43.

27 Letter from Merton to Mark van Doren, 24 February 1966, in Daggy (ed.), *Road to Joy*, p. 50.

28 Letter from Merton to Mark van Doren, 24 February 1966, in Daggy (ed.), *Road to Joy*, p. 51.

29 James Laughlin was the owner and editor of his own publishing house, New Directions Publishing, located in Norfolk, Connecticut. After the publication of Merton's *Thirty Poems*, manuscript sent to

him by Mark van Doren, Laughlin and Merton started a publishing relationship and friendship that lasted until Merton's death. Laughlin, together with Naomi Burton Stone and Brother Patrick Hart, edited *The Asian Journal of Thomas Merton* after Merton's death. For a selection of letters between Laughlin and Merton see David D. Cooper (ed.), *Thomas Merton and James Laughlin: Selected Letters* (New York: Norton), 1997; and a review of those letters in William H. Shannon, Christine M. Bochen and Patrick F. O'Connell (eds), *The Thomas Merton Encyclopedia* (Maryknoll, NY: Orbis), 2002, pp. 474–5. For Laughlin's full biography see *Thomas Merton Encyclopedia*, pp. 248–9.

30 Letter from Merton to Mark van Doren, 18 February 1962, in Daggy (ed.), *Road to Joy*, p. 44.

31 Letter from Merton to Mark van Doren, 29 March 1962, in Daggy (ed.), *Road to Joy*, p. 44.

32 Letter from Merton to Mark van Doren, 9 August 1962, in Daggy (ed.), *Road to Joy*, p. 45.

33 Letter from Merton to Mark van Doren, 19 December 1964, in Daggy (ed.), *Road to Joy*, p. 49.

34 14 March 1968 in Patrick Hart OCSO (ed.), *The Other Side of the Mountain: The Journals of Thomas Merton*, vol. 7, 1967–8 (New York: HarperCollins), 1998, p. 66.

35 Thomas Merton, *The Literary Essays of Thomas Merton* (New York: New Directions), 1981.

36 Lawrence S. Cunningham, *Thomas Merton and the Monastic Vision* (Grand Rapids, MI and Cambridge: William B. Eerdmans), 1999, p. 205.

37 12 November 1967 in Hart (ed.), *Other Side of the Mountain*, p. 11.

38 25 November 1967 in Hart (ed.), *Other Side of the Mountain*, p. 15.

39 12 December 1967 in Hart (ed.), *Other Side of the Mountain*, p. 23.

40 Letter from Merton to Suzanne Butorovich, 22 June 1967 in Daggy (ed.), *Road to Joy*, p. 309.

41 Letter from Merton to Nancy Fly Bredenberg, 11 December 1967 in Daggy (ed.), *Road to Joy*, p. 361.

42 Letter from Merton to Robert Menchin, 15 January 1966 in Shannon (ed.), *Witness to Freedom*, p. 255.

43 Letter from Merton to John Hunt, 18 December 1966 in Shannon (ed.), *Witness to Freedom*, pp. 329–30.

44 *Monks Pond* (Lexington, KY: University of Kentucky Press), 1989.

45 Letter from Merton to Mark van Doren, 12 March 1968 in Daggy (ed.), *Road to Joy*, p. 52.

46 Letter from Merton to Mark van Doren, 13 July 1968 in Daggy (ed.), *Road to Joy*, p. 54.

47 Letter from Merton to Mark van Doren, 12 March 1968 in Daggy (ed.), *Road to Joy*, p. 53, cf. Thomas Merton, *The Collected Poems of Thomas Merton* (New York: New Directions), 1977.

48 Letter from Merton to Mark van Doren, 12 April 1968 in Daggy (ed.), *Road to Joy*, p. 53.

49 9 March 1968 in Hart (ed.), *Other Side of the Mountain*, pp. 63–4.

50 Letter from Merton to Allan Forbes Jr, August 1962 in Shannon (ed.), *Witness to Freedom*, p. 61.

51 Letter from Merton to Allan Forbes Jr, August 1962 in Shannon (ed.), *Witness to Freedom*, p. 61.

52 'A Christmas Letter – 1965' in Daggy (ed.), *Road to Joy*, p. 91.

53 'A Christmas Letter – 1965' in Daggy (ed.), *Road to Joy*, p. 91.

54 John Eudes Bamberger OCSO, *Thomas Merton: Prophet of Renewal* (Kalamazoo, MI: Cistercian Publications), 2005, pp. 25–6.

55 Bamberger OCSO, *Thomas Merton: Prophet of Renewal*, p. 26.

56 Bamberger OCSO, *Thomas Merton: Prophet of Renewal*, pp. 29–30.

57 16 March 1968 in Hart (ed.), *Other Side of the Mountain*, p. 68.

3 Writer and activist

1 Poems available in Lynn R. Szabo (ed.), *In the Dark before Dawn: New Selected Poems of Thomas Merton* (New York: New Directions), 2005, pp. 133–7.

2 Michael Mott, *The Seven Mountains of Thomas Merton* (London: SPCK), 1986, pp. 389–90.

3 'Paschal Time 1968' in Robert E. Daggy (ed.), *The Road to Joy: The Letters of Thomas Merton to New and Old Friends* (New York: Farrar, Straus & Giroux), 1989, p. 113.

4 Daggy (ed.), *Road to Joy*, p. 114.

5 Three important works to understand the history of the Berrigan family and Dan Berrigan's life are Murray Polner and Jim O'Grady, *Disarmed and Dangerous: The Radical Lives and Times of Daniel and Philip Berrigan* (New York: Basic Books), 1997; Daniel Berrigan, *To Dwell in Peace: An Autobiography* (San Francisco: Harper & Row), 1987; and John Dear (ed.), *Apostle of Peace: Essays in Honor of Daniel*

Berrigan (Maryknoll, NY: Orbis), 1996. Philip Berrigan (1923–2002) was ordained as a Josephite priest in late spring 1955 at a liturgical celebration that took place at the Shrine of the Immaculate Conception in Washington, DC, and immediately took up his ministry as assistant pastor at Our Lady of Perpetual Help parish in the Anacostia district working with poor Afro-Americans living in very poor housing; see Polner and O'Grady, *Disarmed and Dangerous*, p. 95. In 1970 Philip Berrigan married Elizabeth McAlister, an activist sister of the Sacred Heart of Mary. They had three children: Frida (born 1 April 1974), Jerry (born 17 April 1975) and Kate (5 November 1981); see Philip Berrigan and Elizabeth McAlister, *The Time's Discipline: The Beatitudes and Nuclear Resistance* (Baltimore, MD: Fortkamp), 1989; and Philip Berrigan with Fred A. Wilcox, *Fighting the Lamb's War: Skirmishes with the American Empire* (Monroe, ME: Common Courage Press), 1996.

6 Lawrence S. Cunningham, *Thomas Merton and the Monastic Vision* (Grand Rapids, MI and Cambridge: William B. Eerdmans), 1999, p. 88. On Daniel Berrigan and Thomas Merton see 'Daniel Berrigan SJ' in Mario I. Aguilar, *Contemplating God, Changing the World* (London: SPCK), 2008, ch. 3, pp. 28–40.

7 Mott, *Seven Mountains of Thomas Merton*, p. 377.

8 One hundred and eleven of these letters were published in William H. Shannon (ed.), *Witness to Freedom: The Letters of Thomas Merton in Times of Crisis* (San Diego, New York and London: Harcourt Brace & Company), 1995, pp. 22–69.

9 Shannon (ed.), *Witness to Freedom*, p. 17.

10 Pope John XXIII, *Pacem in Terris: Encyclical of John XXIII on Establishing Universal Peace in Truth, Justice, Charity and Liberty*, 11 April 1963.

11 Pope John XXIII wrote: 'Hence justice, right reason, and the recognition of man's dignity cry out insistently for a cessation to the arms race. The stock-piles of armaments which have been built up in various countries must be reduced all round and simultaneously by the parties concerned. Nuclear weapons must be banned.' *Pacem in Terris* § 112.

12 'The Cold War Letters: Preface' in Shannon (ed.), *Witness to Freedom*, pp. 19–22, at p. 21.

13 Letter by Thomas Merton to Maynard Shelly, editor of *The Mennonite*, December 1961 in Shannon (ed.), *Witness to Freedom*, pp. 22–3, at p. 23.

14 Cold War Letter 9, from Thomas Merton to Archbishop Thomas Roberts SJ, December 1961 in Shannon (ed.), *Witness to Freedom*, pp. 24–5, at p. 24.

15 Cold War Letter 13, from Thomas Merton to Josiah G. Chatham, December 1961 in Shannon (ed.), *Witness to Freedom*, pp. 25–6, at p. 25.

16 Cold War Letter 17, from Thomas Merton to Clare Booth Luce of New York, December 1961 or January 1962 in Shannon (ed.), *Witness to Freedom*, pp. 26–7, at p. 26.

17 Cold War Letter 18, from Thomas Merton to Walter Stein of Leeds, December 1961 or January 1962 in Shannon (ed.), *Witness to Freedom*, pp. 27–9, at p. 28.

18 Merton's Open Letter to the American Hierarchy, September 1965 in Shannon (ed.), *Witness to Freedom*, pp. 88–94, at p. 94.

19 For a history of the Vietnam war see Stanley Karnow, *Vietnam: A History* (London: Pimlico), revised edition 1994.

20 Mott, *Seven Mountains of Thomas Merton*, p. 383.

21 Mott, *Seven Mountains of Thomas Merton*, p. 383.

22 Mott, *Seven Mountains of Thomas Merton*, p. 384.

23 Merton wrote: '[I]t has become "normal" to regard war – any war demanded by the military – as Christian duty, Christian love, Christian virtue, that a few like the Berrigans, in their desperation, try to show by extreme protest that it is not normal at all'; Circular Letter to Friends Midsummer 1968 in Daggy (ed.), *Road to Joy*, p. 116. Daniel Berrigan's visit was reported in a letter to Sister Therese Lentfoehr SDS, 20 September 1962; see Circular Letter to Friends Midsummer 1968 in Daggy (ed.), *Road to Joy*, p. 241.

24 Thomas Merton, Circular Letter to Friends Midsummer 1968 in Daggy (ed.), *Road to Joy*, p. 116.

25 Letters from Merton to Sister Therese Lentfoehr SDS, 20 December 1962 and 19 February 1963 in Daggy (ed.), *Road to Joy*, p. 243.

26 Letter from Merton to Sister Therese Lentfoehr SDS, 19 February 1963 in Daggy (ed.), *Road to Joy*, p. 243.

27 On hearing the news of Merton's death Dan Berrigan 'wept inconsolably for his dear friend and teacher' in Polner and O'Grady, *Disarmed and Dangerous*, p. 211.

28 Polner and O'Grady, *Disarmed and Dangerous*, p. 107. According to Merton's diary the retreat took place in November 1964 rather than March 1965 as reported by Polner and O'Grady; see entries for 17 and 19 November 1964 in Robert E. Daggy (ed.), *Dancing in the Water*

of Life: Seeking Peace in the Hermitage – The Journals of Thomas Merton, vol. 5, 1963–5 (New York: HarperCollins), pp. 167–8.

29 Mott, *Seven Mountains of Thomas Merton*, pp. 406–7.

30 Mott, *Seven Mountains of Thomas Merton*, p. 407.

31 Daggy (ed.), *Dancing in the Water of Life*, p. 253.

32 Paul R. Dekar, 'Thomas Merton, Gandhi, the "Uprising" of Youth in the '60s, and Building Non-Violent Movements Today', *The Merton Seasonal* 31 (2006/4), pp. 16–23, at p. 21.

33 See David Howard-Pitney, *Martin Luther King, Malcolm X and the Civil Rights Struggle of the 1950s and 1960s* (Boston and New York: Bedford and St Martin's Press), 2004; Malcolm X, *The Autobiography of Malcolm X* (New York: Ballantine Books), 1999; and Michael Eric Dyson, *Making Malcolm: The Myth and Meaning of Malcolm X* (New York: Oxford University Press), 1995. On student demonstrations against the Vietnam war see Kenneth J. Heineman, *Campus Wars: The Peace Movement at American State Universities in the Vietnam Era* (New York: New York University Press), 1993; and for a general analysis of possible contra-narratives see Gerard J. De Groot, *A Noble Cause? America and the Vietnam War* (Harlow: Longman), 2000.

34 The first Buddhist monk to immolate himself was Quang Duc, a 62-year-old who immolated himself in the streets of Saigon in 1963 and left a note requesting 'charity and compassion' from the authorities.

35 See 11 November 1965 in Daggy (ed.), *Dancing in the Water of Life*, p. 314.

36 Merton's diary entry for 7 November 1965 in Daggy (ed.), *Dancing in the Water of Life*, p. 313.

37 Polner and Grady, *Disarmed and Dangerous*, pp. 196–8.

38 For a full narrative of this protest see Daniel Berrigan, *The Trial of the Catonsville Nine* (Boston: Beacon), 1970.

39 17 May 1968 in Patrick Hart OCSO (ed.), *The Other Side of the Mountain: The Journals of Thomas Merton*, vol. 7, 1967–8 (New York: HarperCollins), 1998, p. 103.

40 4 May 1968 in Hart (ed.), *Other Side of the Mountain*, p. 87.

41 8 February 1968 in Hart (ed.), *Other Side of the Mountain*, p. 51.

42 8 February 1968 in Hart (ed.), *Other Side of the Mountain*, p. 52.

43 Thomas Merton, Circular Letter to Friends, midsummer 1968 in Daggy (ed.), *Road to Joy*, p. 116.

44 'Midsummer 1968' in Daggy (ed.), *Road to Joy*, p. 116.

45 John Dear SJ, *Peace Behind Bars: A Peacemaking Priest's Journal from Jail* (Franklin, WI: Sheed & Ward), 1999, p. 3.

46 Mott, *Seven Mountains of Thomas Merton*, p. xxv.

4 Hermit and activist

1 Robert E. Daggy (ed.), *The Road to Joy – The Letters of Thomas Merton to New and Old Friends* (New York: Farrar, Straus & Giroux), 1989, p. 111.

2 28 November 1967 in Patrick Hart OCSO (ed.), *The Other Side of the Mountain: The Journals of Thomas Merton*, vol. 7, 1967–8 (New York: HarperCollins), 1998, p. 17.

3 Lawrence S. Cunningham, *Thomas Merton and the Monastic Vision* (Grand Rapids, MI and Cambridge: William B. Eerdmans), 1999, p. 147.

4 *Perfectae Caritatis* (PC): 'Decree on the Up-To-Date Renewal of Religious Life', 28 October 1965; Paul VI, *Ecclesiae Sanctae* II: 'Norms for Implementing the Decree On the Up-To-Date Renewal of Religious Life', 6 August 1966 and SCRSI, *Renovationis Causam*: 'Instruction on the Renewal of Religious Life', 6 January 1969.

5 PC § 7.

6 PC § 7.

7 24 December 1967 in Hart (ed.), *Other Side of the Mountain*, p. 30.

8 SCRSI, *Venite Seorsum* (VS): 'Instruction on the Contemplative Life and on the Enclosure of Nuns', 15 August 1969.

9 Letter from Merton to a Religious, 30 December 1964 in William H. Shannon (ed.), *Witness to Freedom: The Letters of Thomas Merton in Times of Crisis* (San Diego, New York and London: Harcourt Brace & Company), 1994, pp. 194–5, at p. 194. See for example 'Norms Regulating Papal Enclosure of Nuns', VS VII, § 1–17.

10 7 December 1967 in Hart (ed.), *Other Side of the Mountain*, p. 20, n. 8.

11 See 'Vatican Council, the Second', in William H. Shannon, Christine M. Bochen and Patrick F. O'Connell (eds), *The Thomas Merton Encyclopedia* (Maryknoll, NY: Orbis), 2002, pp. 503–8.

12 Thomas Merton, 'Open Letter to the American Hierarchy', published in the September 1965 issue of *Worldview* and reproduced in Shannon (ed.), *Witness to Freedom*, pp. 88–92, at p. 92.

13 Cunningham, *Thomas Merton and the Monastic Vision*, p. 152.

14 Thomas Merton, *Contemplation in a World of Action* (Notre Dame, IN: University of Notre Dame Press), 1999.

15 Cunningham, *Thomas Merton and the Monastic Vision*, p. 170.

16 Cunningham, *Thomas Merton and the Monastic Vision*, p. 171.

17 Naomi Burton Stone, Brother Patrick Hart and James Laughlin (eds), *The Asian Journal of Thomas Merton* (New York: New Directions), 1975.

18 For the biographies of Dom Flavian and Dom James see 'Burns, Thomas (Fr. Flavian)' and 'Fox, James' in *Thomas Merton Encyclopedia*, pp. 35, 160–1.

19 See 'Carthusians' in *Thomas Merton Encyclopedia*, pp. 42–3.

20 For a series of essays on the spirituality and history of the Camaldolese see Peter Damian Belisle OSB Cam. (ed.), *The Privilege of Love: Camaldolese Benedictine Spirituality* (Collegeville, MN: Liturgical Press), 2002.

21 See 'Camaldolese' in *Thomas Merton Encyclopedia*, pp. 40–1.

22 'Fox, James' in *Thomas Merton Encyclopedia*, p. 160.

23 Letter from Merton to Sister Therese Lentfoehr SDS, 16 June 1965 in Daggy (ed.), *Road to Joy*, p. 251.

24 Michael Mott, *The Seven Mountains of Thomas Merton* (London: SPCK), 1984, p. 424.

25 *Catechism of the Catholic Church* (London: Geoffrey Chapman), 1994, § 920.

26 Merton had written some studies on St Bernard, collected in the book *Thomas Merton on St. Bernard*, Cistercian Studies Series § 9 (Kalamazoo, MI: Cistercian Publications and London and Oxford: A. R. Mowbray), 1980.

27 15 December 1967 in Hart (ed.), *Other Side of the Mountain*, p. 20.

28 Mott, *Seven Mountains of Thomas Merton*, p. 25.

29 For a fruitful exploration of this period see Rob Baker and Gray Henry (eds), *Merton and Sufism, the Untold Story: A Complete Compendium* (Louisville, KY: Fons Vitae), 1999; and Bonnie Thurston, 'Some Reflections on Islamic Poems by Thomas Merton' in Angus Stuart (ed.), *Thomas Merton: The World in my Bloodstream*, Papers from the 2002 Oakham Conference of the Thomas Merton Society of Great Britain and Ireland (Abergavenny: Three Peaks Press), 2004, pp. 40–53.

30 'Aziz, Abdul' in *Thomas Merton Encyclopedia*, p. 20.

31 Mott, *Seven Mountains of Thomas Merton*, p. 432.

32 Mott, *Seven Mountains of Thomas Merton*, p. 432.

33 During 1966 Joan Baez visited Merton and tried to convince him to leave Gethsemani and to join a larger world of peace activism, see Cunningham, *Thomas Merton and the Monastic Vision*, p. 139.

34 21 January 1968 in Hart (ed.), *Other Side of the Mountain*, p. 44.

35 4 January 1968 in Hart (ed.), *Other Side of the Mountain*, p. 33.

36 5 January 1968 in Hart (ed.), *Other Side of the Mountain*, p. 33.

37 Mott, *Seven Mountains of Thomas Merton*, p. 433.

38 Mott, *Seven Mountains of Thomas Merton*, p. 433.

39 For a good biographical historiography of Merton's spiritual development see Cunningham, *Thomas Merton and the Monastic Vision*.

40 The essay appeared in Thomas Merton, *Disputed Questions* (New York: Farrar, Straus & Cudahy), 1960, pp. 177–207, published a year after Pope John XXIII's call for a new Vatican Council. For a commentary on the essay see William R. Shannon, 'Reflections on Thomas Merton's Article: Notes for Philosophy of Solitude', *Cistercian Studies Quarterly* 29 (1994/1).

41 Thomas Merton, *The Way of Chuang Tzu* (New York: New Directions), 1965; *Mystics and Zen Masters* (New York: Farrar, Straus & Company), 1967; and *Zen and the Birds of Appetite* (New York: New Directions), 1968.

42 The three meetings between Merton and the Dalai Lama are described in Merton's diary; see 4–8 November 1968 in Hart (ed.), *Other Side of the Mountain*, pp. 250–66.

43 Letter from Merton to Daniel Clark Walsh, 5 October 1967 in Daggy (ed.), *Road to Joy*, p. 307.

44 A transcription of Merton's talks that were taped were subsequently published as *The Springs of Contemplation* (New York: Farrar, Straus & Giroux), 1992.

45 7 December 1967 in Hart (ed.), *Other Side of the Mountain*, p. 20.

46 4 January 1968 in Hart (ed.), *Other Side of the Mountain*, p. 33.

47 26 January 1968 in Hart (ed.), *Other Side of the Mountain*, pp. 46–7.

48 10 January 1968 in Hart (ed.), *Other Side of the Mountain*, p. 37.

49 Cunningham, *Thomas Merton and the Monastic Vision*, p. 155.

50 14 November 1967 in Hart (ed.), *Other Side of the Mountain*, p. 12.

51 30 December 1967 in Hart (ed.), *Other Side of the Mountain*, p. 31.

52 4 January 1968 in Hart (ed.), *Other Side of the Mountain*, p. 33.

5 Merton and Latin America

1 Michael Mott, *The Seven Mountains of Thomas Merton* (London: SPCK), 1984, p. 458.

2 Malgorzata Poks, *Thomas Merton and Latin America: A Consonance of Voices* (Katowice: Para), 2007, p. 13. The departure of the monks is mentioned by Merton in a letter of 8 October 1966 to Miguel Gringberg, in Christine M. Bochen (ed.), *The Courage for Truth: The Letters of Thomas Merton to Writers* (New York: Farrar, Straus & Giroux), 1993, p. 203.

3 Robert E. Daggy, 'A Man of the Whole Hemisphere: Thomas Merton and Latin America', *American Benedictine Review* 42 (1991/2), p. 124; and Poks, *Thomas Merton and Latin America*, p. 13.

4 Mott, *Seven Mountains of Thomas Merton*; on the visit of Nicanor Parra to Gethsemani see pp. 440–1; on Parra's anti-poetry and his influence on Merton see p. 460.

5 For a recent study of the poetic relation between Merton and Cardenal see Poks, *Thomas Merton and Latin America*, pp. 132–54.

6 I have outlined the history of Nicaragua and Cardenal's history in Mario I. Aguilar, *The History and Politics of Latin American Theology I* (London: SCM Press), 2007, ch. 5.

7 Nicaragua has always been a very literate society and the influence of poets has been central to any national developments; see Thomas W. Walker, *Nicaragua: The Land of Sandino*, 2nd edn (Boulder, CO and London: Westview Press), 1986, pp. 76–7. The same can be said of the influence of left-wing poets within the different periods of possible liberation from oppression; see Bridget Albaraca, Edward Baker, Ileana Rodríguez and Marc Zimmerman (eds), *Nicaragua in Revolution: The Poets Speak/Nicaragua en Revolución: Los Poetas Hablan* (Minneapolis: Marxist Educational Press), 1980.

8 Cardenal asserted: 'Mi principal influencia y mi principal maestro ha sido Ezra Pound' ('Ezra Pound has been my main influence and teacher'), in José Luis González-Balado, *Ernesto Cardenal: Poeta Revolucionario Monje* (Salamanca: Ediciones Sígueme), 1978, p. 58. Ezra Pound (1885–1972) wrote particular aesthetic constructions that included historical assertions in his *Cantos* and also campaigned for the non-intervention of the USA in Italy during the Second World War; see Ira B. Nadel, *Ezra Pound: A Literary Life* (Houndmills and New York: Palgrave Macmillan), 2004.

9 For a comparative textual analysis of Ezra Pound and Cardenal see Eduardo Urdanivia Bertarelli, *La Poesía de Ernesto Cardenal: Cristianismo y Revolución* (Lima: Latinoamericana Editores), 1984, pp. 29–50.

10 Ernesto Cardenal, *Poesía y Revolución: Antología Poética* (Mexico City: Editorial Edicol), 1979, pp. 11–25.

11 Ernesto Cardenal, *Vida perdida: Memorias I* (Madrid: Editorial Trotta), 2005, pp. 99, 102.

12 All Trappist monks take the name Mary as their first name because Mary is the order's patroness; see Jim Forest, *Living with Wisdom: A Life of Thomas Merton* (Maryknoll, NY: Orbis), 1991, p. 79. Cardenal's new name was given in Latin: Laurentius; however, in Spanish Merton used Lorenzo and reminded Cardenal that it was the name of a great writer: D. H. Lawrence; see Cardenal, *Vida perdida*, p. 105.

13 After his departure from Nicaragua, Cardenal's friend Pablo Antonio Cuadra dedicated almost all the literary section of the newspaper *La Prensa* to Ernesto Cardenal; see Cardenal, *Vida perdida*, p. 116.

14 Cardenal, *Vida perdida*, p. 14.

15 Cardenal, *Vida perdida*, pp. 106–7.

16 Cardenal, *Vida perdida*, p. 110.

17 Cardenal, *Vida perdida*, p. 118.

18 Cardenal, *Vida perdida*, p. 112, cf. pp. 137–41; at that time Cardenal's brother Fernando was studying for the priesthood in Ecuador and Merton also asked Ernesto Cardenal to enquire about possible locations for a monastery in Ecuador; Cardenal, *Vida perdida*, pp. 124–5.

19 Cardenal, *Vida perdida*, p. 128.

20 Cardenal, *Vida perdida*, p. 142.

21 *The Rule of Saint Benedict*, trans. Leonard Doyle (Collegeville, MN: Liturgical Press), 2001.

22 Cardenal, *Vida perdida*, pp. 129–30.

23 Cardenal, *Vida perdida*, pp. 145–6.

24 Cardenal, *Vida perdida*, p. 159.

25 Cardenal, *Vida perdida*, pp. 174–5.

26 Cardenal, *Vida perdida*, p. 176.

27 Letter from Thomas Merton to Archbishop Larraona, Head of the Sacred Congregation for Religious at the Vatican, 8 September 1959 in William H. Shannon (ed.), *Witness to Freedom: The Letters of Thomas Merton in Times of Crisis* (San Diego, New York and London: Harcourt Brace & Company), 1994, pp. 205–7.

28 Cardenal, *Vida perdida*, p. 179.

29 Letter from Thomas Merton to Father Jean Daniélou, 5 December 1959 in Shannon (ed.), *Witness to Freedom*, pp. 209–11.

30 Cardenal, *Vida perdida*, p. 284.

31 Letter from Thomas Merton to Ernesto Cardenal, 8 October 1959 in Shannon (ed.), *Witness to Freedom*, pp. 207–9.

32 Cardenal, *Vida perdida*, pp. 263–4; Letter from Thomas Merton to Dom Gregorio Lemercier, 17 December 1959 in Shannon (ed.), *Witness to Freedom*, pp. 211–14.

33 Letter from Thomas Merton to Dom James Fox, 17 December 1959 in Shannon (ed.), *Witness to Freedom*, pp. 214–16.

34 Letter from Thomas Merton to Valerio Cardinal Valeri, 2 January 1960 in Shannon (ed.), *Witness to Freedom*, pp. 216–19.

35 Letter from Thomas Merton to Father Jean Daniélou, 2 January 1960 in Shannon (ed.), *Witness to Freedom*, pp. 219–21.

36 On 17 March 1994 Ernesto Cardenal sent to the editor of Merton's letters three letters that had been given to him by Merton in October 1965 during his visit to Gethsemani. One of these was addressed to Cardenal, another to the Sacred Congregation for Religious in Rome and the third to Pope Paul VI. They were to be sent when and if Merton so wanted, and Cardenal suspected that because his death intervened Merton never had the chance to instruct him to do so. The three letters supported Cardenal's foundation of a monastery in Nicaragua and spoke of the urgent need for contemplative life in Latin America; see Letter from Thomas Merton to Ernesto Cardenal 22 October 1965, Letter from Thomas Merton to the Most Revd Archbishop Paul Philippe and Letter from Thomas Merton to His Holiness Pope Paul VI in Shannon (ed.), *Witness to Freedom*, pp. 227–30.

37 The archipelago of Solentiname has 30 islands and at that time there were around a thousand people or nearly 90 families. Cardenal's lay monastery was located on the largest island, the island of Mancarrón.

38 Claribel Alegría and D. J. Flakoll, *Nicaragua: La Revolución Sandinista – Una crónica política 1855–1979* (Mexico, DF: Ediciones Era), 1982, p. 274.

39 Letter from Merton to Ludovico Silva, 17 January 1966 in Bochen (ed.), *The Courage for Truth*, p. 228.

40 'Yo vine a Solentiname huyendo de lo que tradicionalmente se llama en lenguaje cristiano *el mundo* y que ahora es el capitalismo y la sociedad de consumo. Vine a esta isla buscando la soledad, el silencio, la meditación y, en último término, buscando a Dios. Dios me llevó a los demás hombres. La contemplación me llevó a la revolución. He

dicho otras veces que no fue la lectura de Marx la que me llevó al Marxismo, sino la lectura del evangelio' in González-Balado, *Ernesto Cardenal: Poeta Revolucionario Monje*, p. 152. Translation: 'I came to Solentiname escaping from what is usually called in Christian language *the world* and today is capitalism and the consumerist society. I came to this island searching for solitude, silence, meditation, and ultimately searching for God. God brought me to other people. Contemplation brought me to revolution. I have said many times that it was not reading Marx that brought me to Marxism but reading the Gospel.'

41 Ernesto Cardenal, *El Evangelio en Solentiname* (Salamanca: Ediciones Síagueme), 1976; and *El Evangelio en Solentiname: Volumen Segundo* (Salamanca: Ediciones Síagueme), 1978.

42 Cardenal, 'Introducción' in *El Evangelio en Solentiname*, pp. 9–10.

43 Dinah Livingstone, 'Introduction' in *Nicaraguan New Time: Poems by Ernesto Cardenal* (London: Journeyman), 1998, pp. 11–19, at p. 16.

44 See Bochen (ed.), *Courage for Truth*.

45 Letter from Merton to Nicanor Parra 28 April 1967 in Bochen (ed.), *Courage for Truth*, p. 214.

46 Nicanor Parra, *Poemas & Antipoemas* (Santiago: Editorial Universitaria), 2008.

47 Parra, *Poemas & Antipoemas*, p. 76 (my translation).

48 Letter from Merton to Nicanor Parra, 20 March 1965 in Bochen (ed.), *Courage for Truth*, pp. 212–13, at p. 212.

49 Letter from Merton to Nicanor Parra, 20 March 1965 in Bochen (ed.), *Courage for Truth*, pp. 212–13, at p. 212.

50 Letter from Merton to Nicanor Parra, 12 June 1965 in Bochen (ed.), *Courage for Truth*, pp. 213–14, at p. 213.

51 Poks, *Thomas Merton and Latin America*, p. 201.

52 Paul M. Pearson, 'Poetry of the Sneeze: Thomas Merton and Nicanor Parra', see <http://www.thomasmertonsociety.org/sneeze.htm>.

53 Letter from Merton to Ludovico Silva, 17 January 1966 in Bochen (ed.), *Courage for Truth*, p. 228.

54 Poks, *Thomas Merton and Latin America*, p. 202.

55 Thomas Merton, *Cables to the Ace or Familiar Liturgies of Misunderstanding* (New York: New Directions), 1968.

56 Letter from Merton to Hernán Lavín Cerda, 6 October 1965 in Bochen (ed.), *Courage for Truth*, pp. 212–13, at p. 212.

57 Letter from Merton to Ludovico Silva, 17 January 1966 in Bochen (ed.), *Courage for Truth*, p. 227.

58 Letter from Merton to Cintio Vitier, 6 January 1966 in Bochen (ed.), *Courage for Truth*, p. 240.

59 Letter from Merton to Hernán Lavín Cerda, 20 October 1967 and to Stefan Baciu, 7 July 1966 in Bochen (ed.), *Courage for Truth*, pp. 206, 243.

60 Letter from Merton to Ernesto Cardenal, 2 January 1967 in Bochen (ed.), *Courage for Truth*, p. 158.

61 Letter from Merton to Nicanor Parra, 28 April 1967 in Bochen (ed.), *Courage for Truth*, p. 214.

62 Letter from Merton to Stefan Baciu, 21 May 1965 in Bochen (ed.), *Courage for Truth*, p. 242.

6 Merton's final trip to Asia

1 15 January 1967 in Patrick Hart, OCSO (ed.), *The Other Side of the Mountain: The Journals of Thomas Merton*, vol. 7, 1967–8 (New York: HarperCollins), 1998, pp. 40–3.

2 Michael Casagram OCSO, 'Remembering Father Flavian at Gethsemani: A Reflection at the Memorial Mass for Fr. Flavian Burns OCSO, October 20, 2005', *The Merton Seasonal* 31 (2006/1, Spring), pp. 3–4, at p. 3.

3 After Merton's death the Cistercian leaders of monastic communities who had attended the meeting in Bangkok wrote to Dom Flavian thanking him for allowing Fr Louis (Thomas Merton) to attend the meeting. They mentioned that it had been the attendance and presence of Thomas Merton that had given them enthusiasm to attend the meeting; see Dom Anselm Parker OCSO (Australia), Dom Joachim Murphy OCSO (New Zealand), Dom Simeon Chang OCSO (Hong Kong), Mother Christiana OCSO (Japan), Dom M. F. Acharya OCSO (India) and Dom M. Frans Hardjawijata OCSO (Indonesia), 'Appendix VIII: Letter to Abbot Flavian Burns', 11 December 1968 in Naomi Burton Stone, Brother Patrick Hart and James Laughlin (eds), *The Asian Journal of Thomas Merton* (New York: New Directions), 1975, pp. 344–7.

4 Abbot Robert Barnes OCSO, 'Remembering Father Flavian at Berryville: Homily at the Funeral Mass for Fr. Flavian Burns OCSO, October 17, 2005', *The Merton Seasonal* 31 (2006/1, Spring), pp. 23–5, at p. 24.

5 Brother Patrick Hart, 'Foreword' in *Asian Journal of Thomas Merton*, p. xxii.

6 Vatican II, 'Declaration on the Relation of the Church to Non-Christian Religions', *Nostra Aetate*, 28 October 1965, § 2.

7 *Nostra Aetate*, § 2.

8 See Thomas Merton, 'Appendix IV: Monastic Experience and East-West Dialogue: Notes for a paper to have been delivered at Calcutta, October 1968', *Asian Journal of Thomas Merton*, pp. 309–17, at p. 317; cf. John Eudes Bamberger OCSO, *Thomas Merton: Prophet of Renewal* (Kalamazoo, MI: Cistercian Publications), 2005, p. 18.

9 *Asian Journal of Thomas Merton*, especially 'November Circular Letters to Friends', 9 November 1968, New Delhi, India, pp. 320–5, at pp. 321–3.

10 The Fourteenth Dalai Lama, 'The Nobel Peace Prize Lecture, Oslo, Norway', in Sidney Piburn (ed.), *The Dalai Lama: A Policy of Kindness – An Anthology of Writings by and about the Dalai Lama* (Ithaca, NY: Snow Lion Publications), 1990, pp. 15–25, at p. 15.

11 Hart, 'Foreword' in *Asian Journal of Thomas Merton*, p. xxiii.

12 During the 1960s Merton had corresponded with many scholars of Hinduism and Buddhism; see for example, William Apel, 'There Comes a Time: The Interfaith Letters of Thomas Merton and Dona Luisa Coomaraswamy', *The Merton Journal* 13 (2006/2), pp. 11–18; and William Apel, *Signs of Peace: The Interfaith Letters of Thomas Merton* (Maryknoll, NY: Orbis), 2006.

13 15 October 1968 in *Asian Journal of Thomas Merton*, p. 5.

14 17 October 1968 in *Asian Journal of Thomas Merton*, p. 10.

15 *Asian Journal of Thomas Merton*, p. 14.

16 18 October 1968, *Asian Journal of Thomas Merton*, p. 16.

17 19 October 1968, *Asian Journal of Thomas Merton*, p. 24.

18 *Asian Journal of Thomas Merton*, p. 28.

19 20 October 1968, *Asian Journal of Thomas Merton*, p. 29.

20 *Asian Journal of Thomas Merton*, pp. 30–1.

21 *Asian Journal of Thomas Merton*, pp. 33–4.

22 28 October 1968 in *Asian Journal of Thomas Merton*, p. 54.

23 *Asian Journal of Thomas Merton*, p. 63.

24 *Asian Journal of Thomas Merton*, p. 63.

25 Giuseppe Tucci (1894–1984), an Italian scholar of Tibetan Buddhism who taught all his life at the University La Sapienza in Rome. Merton refers to Tucci's work, *The Theory and Practice of the Mandala* first published in 1949.

26 *Asian Journal of Thomas Merton*, pp. 57–9, 61–3, 66–8, 82–8.

27 *Asian Journal of Thomas Merton*, p. 64.

28 *Asian Journal of Thomas Merton*, p. 64.

29 *Asian Journal of Thomas Merton*, pp. 65–6.

30 *Asian Journal of Thomas Merton*, p. 66.

31 *Asian Journal of Thomas Merton*, p. 70.

32 See 'Talbott, Harold', in William H. Shannon, Christine M. Bochen and Patrick F. O'Connell (eds), *The Thomas Merton Encyclopedia* (Maryknoll, NY: Orbis), 2002, p. 462.

33 *Asian Journal of Thomas Merton*, p. 78.

33 *Asian Journal of Thomas Merton*, p. 92.

35 The Fourteenth Dalai Lama, Tenzin Gyatso, was born into a peasant family in Amdo, eastern Tibet, in 1935 and, after being identified as the incarnation of the previous Dalai Lama at the age of two, he was moved to Lhasa at the age of four. With the Chinese occupation of Tibet the political situation changed, and after the Tibetan National Uprising on 10 March 1959 the Dalai Lama left Tibet and moved to India, where he was given refugee status. Over the years thousands of Tibetan refugees crossed into India and the Dalai Lama managed to establish monasteries as well as his government in Dharamsala, where he met Merton in 1968. For a detailed account of the Dalai Lama's life see Michael Harris Goodman, *The Last Dalai Lama: A Biography* (London: Sidgwick & Jackson), 1986.

36 See Thomas Merton, 'November circular letter to friends', New Delhi, India, 9 November 1968, published as 'Appendix VI' in *Asian Journal of Thomas Merton*, pp. 320–5; Merton's visit is also mentioned in Goodman, *The Last Dalai Lama*, p. 325.

37 *Thomas Merton Encyclopedia* (Maryknoll, NY: Orbis), pp. 98–9, at p. 98.

38 *Asian Journal of Thomas Merton*, p. 100. The same description of the meetings as published in Merton's *Asian Journal* has also been included in the last volume of Merton's personal diaries; see Hart (ed.), *Other Side of the Mountain*, pp. 249–66.

39 *Asian Journal of Thomas Merton*, p. 93.

40 *Asian Journal of Thomas Merton*, p. 94.

41 *Asian Journal of Thomas Merton*, p. 95; full description of the conversation can be found on pp. 93–5.

42 *Asian Journal of Thomas Merton*, p. 96.

43 Wilbur H. Ferry, formerly Vice-President of the Center for the Study of Democratic Institutions (successor to the Fund for the Republic)

in Santa Barbara, California. Ferry was a loyal friend of Merton in the last years of his life and visited him at Gethsemani often; see Thomas Merton to Mr and Mrs Harold Brewster Jenkins, 31 December 1967 in Robert E. Daggy (ed.), *The Road to Joy: The Letters of Thomas Merton to New and Old Friends* (New York: Farrar, Straus & Giroux), 1989, pp. 82–3, at p. 83. When Merton visited California in 1968 he stayed with Ferry and his wife in Santa Barbara and they drove along the coastline; *Asian Journal of Thomas Merton*, p. 175. Ferry brought Merton to the Santa Barbara Center, where Merton engaged in a lively manner with scholars working there. Ferry drove him to different possible sites for a hermitage, which was part of the mission Merton had from his abbot in visiting California; see 'Ferry, Wilbur H.' in *Thomas Merton Encyclopedia*, pp. 154–5.

44 Daisetz Teitaro Suzuki (1870–1966) was a Japanese scholar who interpreted Buddhism, and particularly Zen Buddhism, to the West and Christianity to the East. Merton met him in 1964 when Suzuki lectured at Columbia University; see 'Zen' in *Thomas Merton Encyclopedia*, pp. 546–8.

45 *Asian Journal of Thomas Merton*, pp. 100–1.

46 'November 4/Afternoon' in *Asian Journal of Thomas Merton*, pp. 100–2.

47 *Asian Journal of Thomas Merton*, p. 102.

48 *Asian Journal of Thomas Merton*, p. 102.

49 *Asian Journal of Thomas Merton*, p. 103.

50 *Asian Journal of Thomas Merton*, pp. 107–12.

51 *Asian Journal of Thomas Merton*, pp. 112–13.

52 *Asian Journal of Thomas Merton*, p. 112.

53 *Asian Journal of Thomas Merton*, p. 113.

54 *Asian Journal of Thomas Merton*, p. 113.

55 7 November 1968 in *Asian Journal of Thomas Merton*, p. 117.

56 *Asian Journal of Thomas Merton*, p. 119.

57 *Asian Journal of Thomas Merton*, p. 121.

58 *Asian Journal of Thomas Merton*, pp. 124–5.

59 *Asian Journal of Thomas Merton*, p. 125. On the Dalai Lama and Marxism see the Fourteenth Dalai Lama, *Freedom in Exile: The Autobiography of His Holiness the Dalai Lama of Tibet* (London: Hodder & Stoughton), 1990, pp. 98–9, 251 and particularly p. 296, where he confesses that 'in as much as I have any political allegiance, I suppose I am still half Marxist' and 'the other attractive thing about

Marxism for me is its assertion that man is ultimately responsible for his own destiny. This reflects Buddhist thought exactly.'

60 The Dalai Lama writes about 'Father Thomas Merton, the American Benedictine Monk'; see the Fourteenth Dalai Lama, *Freedom in Exile*, pp. 207–8. See also Joseph Quinn Raab, 'Comrades for Peace: Thomas Merton, The Dalai Lama and the Preferential Option for Nonviolence', in Victor A. Kramer and David Belcastro (eds), *The Merton Annual: Studies in Culture, Spirituality and Social Concerns* 19 (Louisville, KY: Fons Vitae) 2006, pp. 255–66.

61 *Nostra Aetate* § 1, cf. Acts 17.26.

62 Photograph available in *Thomas Merton Encyclopedia*, p. 99.

63 'Dalai Lama (Tenzin Gyatso)', in *Thomas Merton Encyclopedia*, pp. 98–9, at p. 99.

64 Tsong-Kha-Pa, Lam Rim Chen Mo, *The Great Treatise on the Stages of the Path to Enlightenment*, vol. I, IV A 2a, trans. the Lamrim Chenmo Translation Committee, Joshua E. C. Cutler (editor-in-chief) and Guy Newland (ed.) (Ithaca, NY: Snow Lion Publications), 2000, p. 99.

65 This daily practice is made clear in a recent autobiography of a Tibetan woman in exile in Britain when she writes: 'Whatever my work schedule, though, every day I woke up at 4 am to say my prayers and perform my meditation, as I had done since I lived with the Dalai Lama in Dharamsala', in Soname Yangchen with Vicki Mackenzie, *Child of Tibet: The Story of Soname's Flight to Freedom* (London: Portrait), 2007, p. 143.

66 Yangchen with Mackenzie, *Child of Tibet*, p. 143.

67 Merton, 'Appendix IV', pp. 309–17, at p. 316 7§ 9.

68 Merton's newsletter from Calcutta was reproduced after his death as 'Appendix VI: November Circular Letter to Friends' in *Asian Journal of Thomas Merton*, pp. 320–5.

69 Merton, 'Appendix VI', p. 324.

70 *Asian Journal of Thomas Merton*, p. 134.

71 *Asian Journal of Thomas Merton*, p. 135.

72 *Asian Journal of Thomas Merton*, p. 135.

73 *Asian Journal of Thomas Merton*, p. 141.

74 *Asian Journal of Thomas Merton*, p. 142.

Conclusion: Merton's lessons for today

1 Father Louis OCSO (Thomas Merton), 'Marxism and Monastic Activities', talk delivered at Bangkok on 10 December 1968 in Naomi

Burton Stone, Brother Patrick Hart and James Laughlin (eds), *The Asian Journal of Thomas Merton* (New York: New Directions), 1975, pp. 326–43.

2 For a description of Merton's lecture and death in Bangkok see Dom Anselm Parker OCSO (Australia), Dom Joachim Murphy OCSO (New Zealand), Dom Simeon Chang OCSO (Hong Kong), Mother Christiana OCSO (Japan), Dom M. F. Acharya OCSO (India) and Dom M. Frans Hardjawijata OCSO (Indonesia), 'Letter to Abbot Flavian Burns', Sawang Kaniwat, Bangkok, 11 December 1968 in *Asian Journal of Thomas Merton*, pp. 344–7.

3 *Asian Journal of Thomas Merton*, pp. 328–9.

4 *Asian Journal of Thomas Merton*, p. 329.

5 *Asian Journal of Thomas Merton*, p. 329.

6 *Asian Journal of Thomas Merton*, p. 326.

7 *Asian Journal of Thomas Merton*, p. 327.

8 *Asian Journal of Thomas Merton*, p. 327.

9 Herbert Marcuse (1898–1978) was born in Berlin and completed his doctorate at the University of Freiburg in 1922. After a spell in Berlin he returned to Freiburg, where he prepared his habilitation with Martin Heidegger. As he could not complete his project under the Nazis he worked at the Frankfurt Institute for Social Research and emigrated to Switzerland in 1933 and later to the United States, where he became a citizen in 1940. During the Second World War he worked for the US Office of Strategic Services. In 1952 he began his academic career as a political theorist at Columbia, Harvard, Brandeis and the University of California at San Diego. Marcuse engaged himself with the protests of the 1960s and was known as 'the Father of the New Left'. His main works of that time were his synthesis of Marx and Freud, *Eros and Civilization* (1955) and *One-Dimensional Man*, work used by Merton for his lecture.

10 *Asian Journal of Thomas Merton*, p. 335.

11 *Asian Journal of Thomas Merton*, p. 328.

12 *Asian Journal of Thomas Merton*, p. 343.

13 León Gómez Araneda, *Que el pueblo juzgue: Historia del Golpe de Estado* (Santiago, Chile: Terranova Editores), 1988; Ignacio González Camus, *El día en que murió Allende* (Santiago, Chile: CESOC Ediciones Chileamérica), 1988; Paz Rojas, Viviana Uribe, María Eugenia Rojas, Iris Largo, Isabel Ropert and Víctor Espinoza, *Páginas en Blanco: El 11 de septiembre en La Moneda* (Santiago, Chile: Ediciones B Chile),

2001; Robinson Rojas Sandford, *The Murder of Allende and the End of the Chilean Way to Socialism* (New York, Evanston, San Francisco and London: Harper & Row), 1976; and Oscar Soto, *El Ultimo Día de Salvador Allende* (Santiago, Chile: Aguilar Chilena de Ediciones), 1999.

14 Salvador Allende, Last words through Radio Magallanes, Santiago, Chile, 11 September 1973.

15 *Asian Journal of Thomas Merton*, p. 331. Teilhard de Chardin (1881– 1955), Jesuit and trained palaeontologist, took part in the discovery of the Peking man in China. In his book *The Phenomenon of Man* Teilhard abandoned the strict narrative of Genesis as an account for the creation and unfolding of the cosmos and proposed a religious and scientific development of the atmosphere. Teilhard's work was banned by the Vatican because of the implications of his ideas against the doctrine of original sin, and his condemnation was clear in the 1950 encyclical *Humani generis*. In 2009 Pope Benedict XVI praised Teilhard's idea of the universe as a 'living host' but Teilhard's works still carried a warning about his ideas.

16 *Asian Journal of Thomas Merton*, p. 330.

17 *Asian Journal of Thomas Merton*, p. 331.

18 *Asian Journal of Thomas Merton*, p. 332.

19 *Asian Journal of Thomas Merton*, p. 332.

20 *Asian Journal of Thomas Merton*, p. 333.

21 *Asian Journal of Thomas Merton*, p. 333.

22 *Asian Journal of Thomas Merton*, p. 334.

23 *Asian Journal of Thomas Merton*, p. 334.

24 *Asian Journal of Thomas Merton*, p. 334.

25 *Asian Journal of Thomas Merton*, p. 340.

26 Thomas Merton, 'Appendix IX, The Significance of the Bhagavad-Gita', in *Asian Journal of Thomas Merton*, pp. 348–53, at p. 353.

27 Thomas Merton, 'Special Closing Prayer' offered at the First Spiritual Summit Conference in Calcutta by Father Thomas Merton, Appendix V in *Asian Journal of Thomas Merton*, pp. 318–19.

28 Louis Althusser (1918–90) was born in Algeria and studied at the École Normal Supérieure in Paris, where he became a professor of philosophy. He was a Marxist philosopher and a long-time member of the French Communist Party. A structuralist Marxist who challenged any humanism in Marx, he was also critical of the overuse of structures for personality cults and made a passionate defence of

the line exercised by the Chinese Communist Party. In 1980 he strangled his wife and was committed to a mental hospital for three years, losing influence within the French political scene. His major works were on Marxism and on ideology, for example, *Reading Capital* and *Ideology and Ideological State Apparatuses: Notes towards an Investigation.*

29 At the start of his lecture Merton made a personal confession to avoid criticisms of his lack of formal study of Marxism in an age in which more people than now were conversant with Marxism because of its influence in the Soviet Union and the cold war. He said: 'I must apologize for giving you what will inevitably be a rather impressionistic treatment of something I do not know very much about, because I cannot possibly pretend to be an authority in Marxism'; see *Asian Journal of Thomas Merton*, p. 326.

30 *Asian Journal of Thomas Merton*, p. 151.
31 *Asian Journal of Thomas Merton*, pp. 191–209.
32 *Asian Journal of Thomas Merton*, pp. 211–36.
33 *Asian Journal of Thomas Merton*, p. 237.
34 *Asian Journal of Thomas Merton*, p. 238.
35 *Asian Journal of Thomas Merton*, p. 248.
36 *Asian Journal of Thomas Merton*, p. 252.
37 *Asian Journal of Thomas Merton*, p. 252.
38 *Asian Journal of Thomas Merton*, p. 253.
39 *Asian Journal of Thomas Merton*, p. 254.

Index

Agudelo, William 83–4
Aide à l'Implantation Monastique 93
Alacion, Fr (Corrientes) 28
Albert, Dom, Prior of Caldey 20
Alberto, Carlos 83
Alegría, Ciro 28
Allende, Salvador 110, 114
Althusser, Louis 113, 114, 144–5n28
Amayo, Fr (Iquitos) 28
'And the children of Birmingham'
  46–7
'April 4th 1968' 46–7
The Ascent to Truth 68
Asia, Merton's final trip 90–106,
  115–16; meetings with the Dalai
  Lama 97–104, 106; Tibetan
  experience of the stranger 93–5
The Asian Journal of Thomas
  Merton 15, 113
Aziz, Abdul 68, 70

Baez, Joan 69
Baigorri, Angel Martínez 78
Baldwin, Fr 67
Bamberger, John Eudes 14, 44–5
Bangkok 3, 95, 115–16
Barnes, Robert 1
Berrigan, Daniel 47, 48, 51–6, 57,
  58, 59, 129n27
Berrigan, Philip 47, 52–3, 54, 56,
  57, 58, 127–8n5
Bhagavadgītā 113
Blake, William 43

Breakthrough to Peace 39
Buddhism 57, 92, 93, 94; and
  Marxism 111–12; Tibetan see
  Tibetan Buddhism; Zen 72, 94
Burns, Flavian 65, 90–1, 105, 138n3
Butorovich, Suzanne 42

Cables to the Ace 88
Calcutta 95
Camaldolese Benedictines 65, 66
Camus, Albert 40, 44
Canedo, Antonio 28
Capovilla, Monsignor Loris 35
Cardenal, Ernesto 17, 23–4, 27, 30,
  77–85, 134n8, 135n12, 135n18,
  136n36, 136–7n40
Cardenal, Fernando 135n18
Carthusians 65–6
Casagram, Michael 90
Catholic Peace Fellowship 55
Catholic Worker 48
civil rights 46–7, 55
Clement, Brother 34
cold war 43
Collins, Frederic 75
Columbia University 4–5, 9, 38
Conjectures of a Guilty Bystander 8, 11
contemplation: in daily life 115–16;
  and human activity 108–13;
  as life 74–5; Merton as a
  contemplative see under Merton,
  Thomas; and nuclear weapons
  48–51; and the philosophy of

solitude 70–3; and political activity 113–15; and social text 13–15; and the Vietnam war 51–8; Zen 72
Cornell, Tom 54
Covarrubias, Miguel 27
Cuadra, Pablo Antonio 29–30, 78, 80, 83, 124n52
Cuernavaca monastery 30, 67, 82
Cunnane, Robert 54
Cunningham, Lawrence 40, 48, 75

Daggy, Robert 77
Dalai Lama, Tenzin Gyatso, Fourteenth 73, 92–3, 97–104, 106, 140n35, 141–2nn59–60
Daniélou, Jean 82, 83
Darjeeling 105–6
Day, Dorothy 48
Dear, John 59
death row prisoners 21–2
Delhi 96–7, 105
Dharamsala 97–102
Disputed Questions 36, 133n40
Douglass, Jim 54
Dylan, Bob 69
dzogchen 100

emptiness (*sunyata*) 72, 99, 103
Enrique, Jesus 28

Ferman (school teacher) 28
Fernandes, Fr (Lima) 28
Ferry, W. H. ('Ping') 54, 100, 140–1n43
Flavian, Dom (Flavian Burns) 65, 90–1, 105, 138n3
Forest, Jim 3, 48, 54
Fox, James 48, 65
Fredriksson, Lynn 59
French Marxism 113–14

Friedrich, Bruce 59
Furlong, Monica 5

Gabriel, Dom 20
Gandhi, Mahatma 35, 48
Gangon, Josué 28
García (Buenos Aires) 28
Geshe, Tenzin 99
Gethsemani, Abbey of 3, 6–7; manual work 19; master of scholastics' role 18; Merton's criticisms of 20, 25; Merton's hermitage 15, 34–5, 39, 67, 68–70
Gomes (Rio de Janeiro) 28
Grady, John Peter 54
Gyaltsan, Geshe Tenpa 96

Hart, Patrick 93, 105
hermits 62–7, 72; Merton as hermit and activist 61–75
Herz, Alice 55
Hugo, Fr (Costa Rica) 28
Hunt, John 43

James, Dom 'Edelin' 61, 66, 67
Jaramillo, Fray 28
Jaramillo, Guillermo 28
Jean, Elbert F. 54
Jenkins, Ruth 4
Jesus Christ 1, 73
John XXIII 10, 48–9, 51, 128n11
Johnson, Lyndon B. 55, 57
José, Fr 22
Joyce, James 43

Kelly, Timothy 102
Kennedy, John F. 49
Khantipalo, Phra 95
Khempo of Namgyal Tra-Tsang 99

King, Martin Luther 46–7
Kirk, Grayson 38–9
Kramer, Victor A. 35

Laporte, Roger 55
Larraona, Cardinal 30, 34
Latin America 25–8, 29–30, 67,
    76–89, 136n36
Laughlin, James 39, 86, 88,
    125–6n29
Leclercq, Jean 66, 115
Lemercier, Gregorio 25, 30, 81, 82
Lévi-Strauss, Claude 41
Lhalungpa, Lobsang Phuntsok 96
Lima, Jorge de 27
Literary Essays of Thomas Merton
    40
Louf, André 65
Luce, Clare Boothe 50

'M' (nurse) 41, 77
McDole, Bob 54
Malcolm X 55
mandalas 96
Marcuse, Herbert 108–10, 143n9
Maritain, Jacques 5, 85
Marxism 84, 102, 108–15,
    141–2n59, 144–5nn28–9;
    French 113–14
Massignon, Louis 68
meditation, Tibetan Buddhist 101,
    103–4, 142n65
Menchin, Robert 42
Merton, Owen 4
Merton, Thomas: anti-poetry as
    influence on 85–9; Asian trip *see*
    Asia, Merton's final trip; and
    Cardenal 17, 23–4, 27, 30, 77–85,
    135n12, 135n18, 136n36; and
    civil rights 46–7, 55; and

Columbia University 4–5, 9, 38;
    as a contemplative activist 1–16,
    107–15, 108–13; contemplative
    political writings 7–8, 43–4,
    46–60; as a contemplative
    teacher 17–31; as a
    contemplative writer 7–8, 32–45;
    as a contradictory writer 43–5;
    conversion to Catholicism 4–5;
    daily contemplation of 115–16;
    and the Dalai Lama 97–104, 106,
    142n60; death 2–3, 106, 108;
    formal commitment to hermit
    life 40; as a free writer 42–3;
    funeral 2; gradual change to
    become a pilgrim 13–15; as
    hermit and activist 61–75; and
    Latin America 25–8, 29–30, 67,
    76–89, 136n36; legacy of lessons
    for today 115–17; life overview
    4–7; love of diversity 116–17;
    and Marxism 102, 108–15,
    145n29; as master of scholastics
    8, 20–2; monastic learning of
    17–20; monastic vows 8; as
    novice master 8, 23–31; and
    nuclear weapons 47, 48–51;
    philosophy of solitude 70–5;
    prayer 18–19, 68–70; published
    writings discussed *see specific
    titles*; rejection of becoming a
    product 116; schooling 4, 9; and
    the stranger *see* strangers; and
    the Vietnam war 44, 47, 51–8,
    51–60, 74; vocation and entering
    Gethsemani 6–7; as writer and
    activist 46–60; as a writer to
    others 34, 40–2
Mexican Journal of Literature 27
Mistral, Gabriela 27

Index

Le Monde 99–100
Monks Pond magazine 43
Montaldo, Jonathan 13
Morrison, Norman 55
Mott, Michael 2
Muste, A. J. 54

Nechiung Rimpoche 97
Nelson, John Oliver 54
Neruda, Pablo 27, 78
New Seeds of Contemplation 52
'Notes for a philosophy of solitude'
    70–1
nuclear weapons 47, 48–51,
    128n11

Ocampo, Victoria 52–3, 85
Orchard, Bernard 14
'Original Child Bomb' 88

Parra, Nicanor 77, 85, 86–8
Paul VI 64–5, 136n36
Peace in the Post-Christian Era 39,
    49
peace movement 44, 47, 56–8, 69
Pearl Harbour 6
Pearson, Paul 88
Pérez, Rigoberto López 78
'Picture of a black child with a
    white doll' 46–7
Poks, Malgorzata 76–7, 88
political activity: contemplation
    and 113–15; Merton's
    contemplative political writings
    7–8, 43–4, 46–60
Porion, Jean-Baptiste 65
Pound, Ezra 134n8

Quainton, Anthony and Mrs 96
Quang Duc, Thich 130n34

Rampa, Lobsang 28–9
Revista Mexicana de Literatura
    (*Mexican Journal of Literature*)
    27
Reyes, Alfonso 27
Ricaurte, Monsignor (Bogotá) 28
Rodutskey, Andrew 18

The Secular Journal 29
The Seven Storey Mountain 4, 6, 53,
    62, 80
Shannon, Bill 48
sign language 25, 79
The Sign of Jonas 7, 8, 14, 19–20
The Silent Life 66
Silva, Ludovico, correspondence
    with Merton 83, 85, 88
Solentiname 83–5, 136n37,
    136–7n40
solitude 2, 35, 61, 63, 64; Merton's
    struggle/search for 8, 20, 24, 25,
    60, 62, 94; philosophy of 70–3
Sopa, Geshe 100
Sortais, Gabriel 48, 49
Sourain (Viña del Mar) 28
Spellman, Cardinal 56
Stein, Walter 50–1
strangers: Merton's destruction of
    the stranger 102–5; Merton's
    ecclesial experience of the
    stranger 9–13; Merton's Tibetan
    experience of the stranger 93–4;
    the stranger in Merton 9
Suzuki, D. T. 100, 141n44

Talbott, Harold 96, 97, 99, 100
Teilhard de Chardin, Pierre 111,
    144n15
Thicchen Rimpoche, Chobgye 101–2
Thomas Aquinas 5

Thugsey Rimpoche, Drugpa 106
Tibetan Buddhism 28–9, 73, 98,
    100, 101, 103 (*see also* Dalai
    Lama, Tenzin Gyatso,
    Fourteenth); meditation 101,
    103–4, 142n65
Tobin, Sr Mary Luke 64
Trungpa Rimpoche, Chogyam 95
Tseten, Geshe Ugyen 100
Tsong-Kha-Pa 103

United Fruit Company 27
Urrea, Monsignor (Santa Rosa de
    Osos) 28
Urtecho, José Coronel 78, 83

Valeri, Cardinal Valerio 30
Vallejo, César 78
van Doren, Charles (Charlie) 36,
    37

van Doren, Dorothy 36
van Doren, John 36
van Doren, Mark 23–4, 36–7, 38,
    43; Merton's letters to 19–20, 21,
    23, 38, 39
Vander Vennett, Timothy 18
Vatican Council II 10, 11, 12–13, 25,
    49, 51, 91–2; and hermits 62–7
Vietnam war 44, 47, 51–8, 74, 94

Walsh, Anthony 54
Walsh, Dan 5
The Waters of Siloe 66
Waugh, Evelyn 85
Wolfer, Vianney 18

Yangchen, Soname 103
Yoder, John H. 54

Zen 72, 94